Finally, we've discovered how to fit a canyon, a mesa, a gulf, and a desert into any classroom.

With SRA Geography, you can integrate geography lessons with any social studies curriculum.

Grade 3

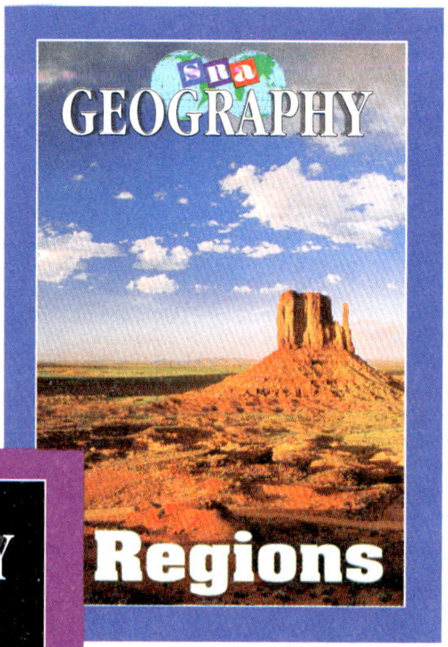

Grade 4

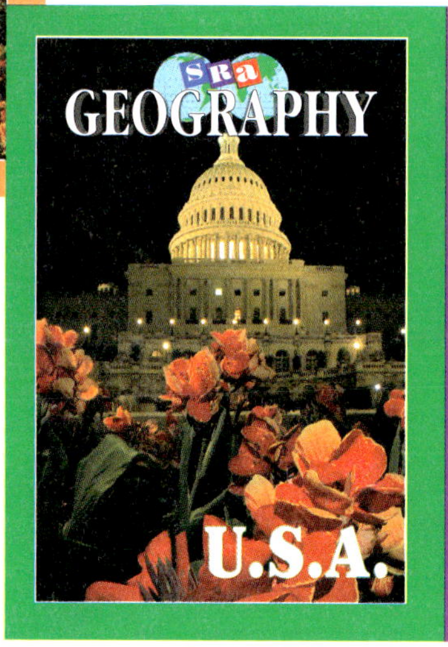

Grade 5

Grade 6

Chances are you've heard all about how high school students can't find Washington, D.C., on a map. You've heard about the Geography Standards and you've read about the five fundamental themes and the five basic skills of geography. You've heard about the countless studies that led to the development of those standards—studies that reported a shocking lack of fundamental geography skills among students across this country.

You also know how difficult it can be to fit geography lessons into an already-crowded 3–6 grade curriculum.

Now SRA has created a program that gives your students the geography knowledge that's essential for future success.

SRA Geography

Taking a more down-to-earth approach to understanding the world.

With ***SRA Geography*** you can help your students understand the cause-and-effect relationship that exists between people and the places they call home. They'll understand that geography is about much more than pinpointing places on a map: it's about understanding how the land can put its mark on people—one river, lake, mountain, or volcano at a time.

Designed for grades 3–6, ***SRA Geography*** is the program that aligns perfectly with the four social studies topics you're already teaching: **communities, states and regions, United States history,** and **world history.**

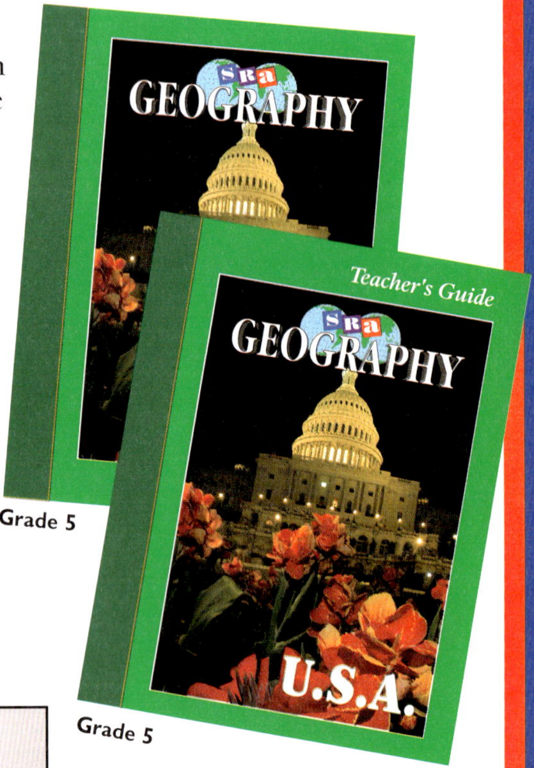

Grade 5

Grade 5

SRA Geography consists of the following components:

- **Student Activity Book**
  includes 18 three-part lessons so you can strengthen geography knowledge and skills every two weeks in your social studies curriculum.
- **Annotated Teacher's Guide**
  includes background information, objectives, strategies, and resource correlations so you can prepare for each lesson in the time it takes to open your book.
- **Supplemental Resources**
  created by the National Geographic Society help you fill in all the details in a high-interest, engaging format.

For more information about SRA products, to place an order, or to follow up on your order, please call SRA Customer Service toll-free at 1-888/SRA-4KIDS (1-888/772-4543), from 8 A.M. to 7 P.M., Eastern Time.

SRA

GEOGRAPHY

Communities

Teacher's Guide

AUTHORS

James F. Marran
Social Studies Chair Emeritus
New Trier Township High School
Winnetka, Illinois

Cathy L. Salter
Geography Teacher
Educational Consultant
Hartsburg, Missouri

Teacher's Guide
Table of Contents

SRA
McGraw-Hill
Columbus, Ohio

A Division of The McGraw·Hill Companies

Each individual element is simply out of this world.

Student Activity Book

These full-color activity books reach out and involve students in geographic questions and decision making with

- 18 six-page lessons that align with social studies curriculum,
- a 24-page Almanac filled with reference information collected in maps, charts, graphs, and tables, and
- a glossary of key geographical terms

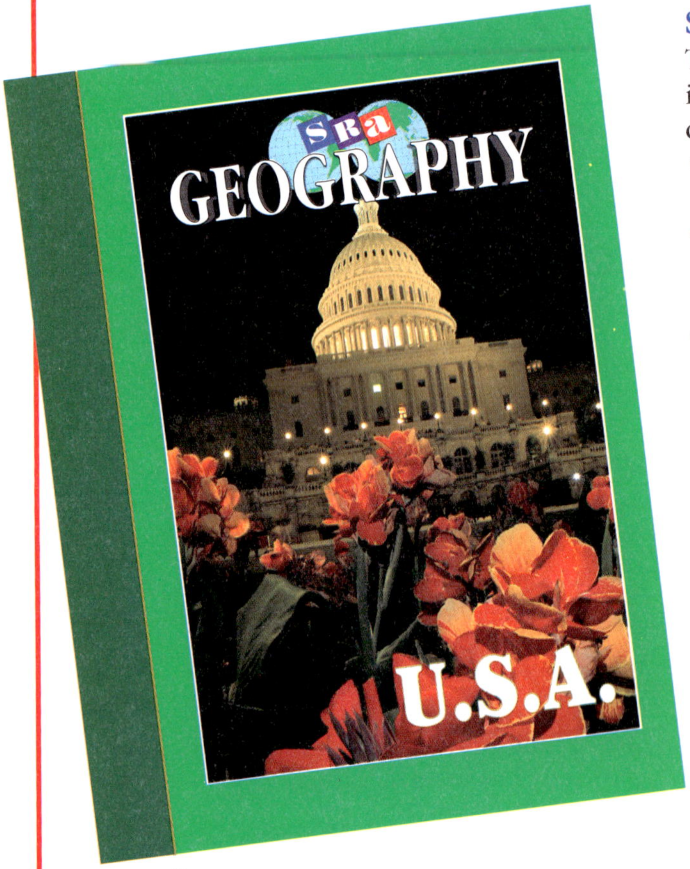

Grade 5

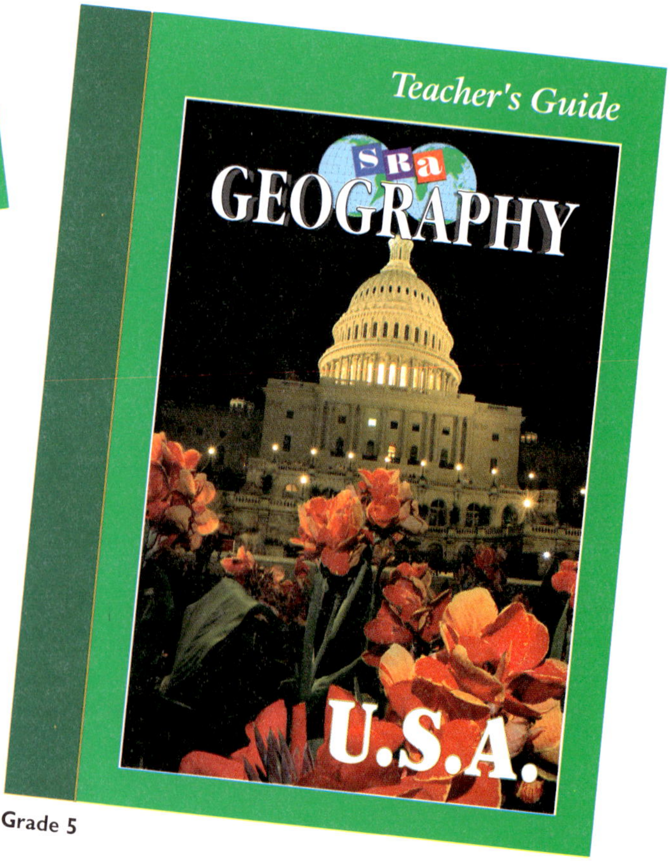

Grade 5

Teacher's Guide

This overprinted, annotated version of the student book provides

- comprehensive teacher support for each lesson
- a professional handbook that includes professional development articles and information about geography and the geography standards
- Standardized Test-Format Assessment masters

Let the National Geographic Society help bring the world to your classroom.

Program Resources

Learn More About It

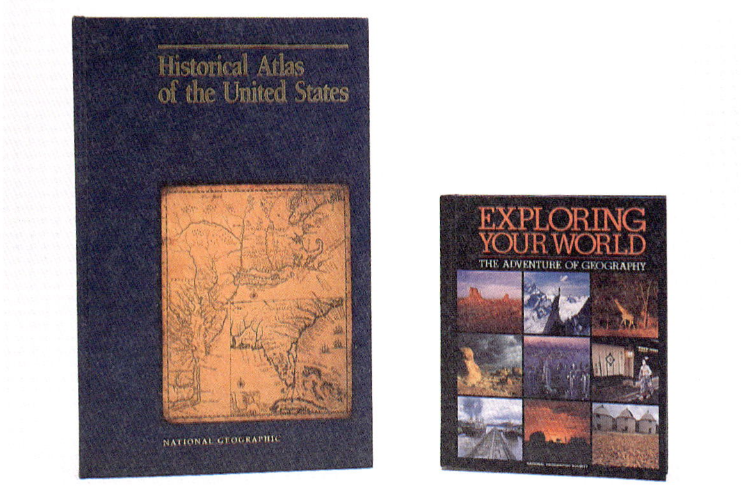

National Geographic Society resources are all referenced with appropriate lessons in the Teacher's Guide, so you can integrate materials easily, right when you need them. The Program Resources are available through SRA by calling the Customer Service toll-free number 1-888/SRA-4KIDS (1-888/772-4543). The Learn More About It resources can be ordered from National Geographic directly at 1-800/368-2728, or may be available at your local library.

Cover the highs and lows of the world in 18 simple steps.

The 18 lessons in each Student Activity Book help you cover all the high points in your community, your state, the United States, and the world.

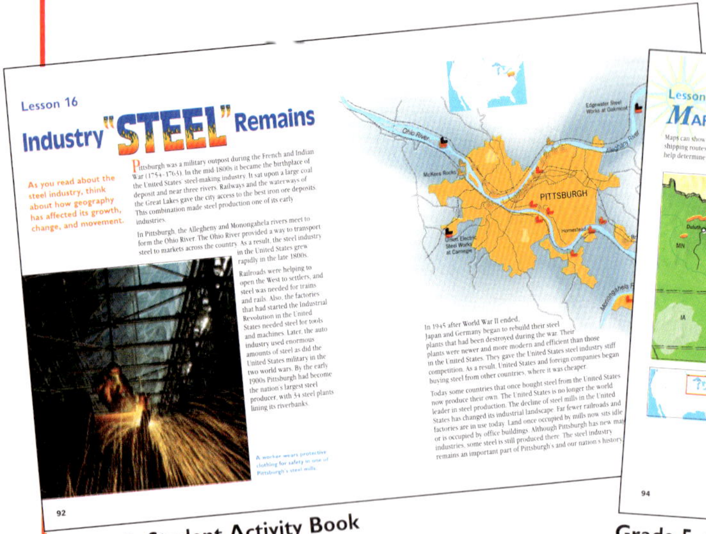

Grade 5, Student Activity Book

Two-page informational article uses colorful photographs and student-friendly text to introduce students to a new place and describe some of the geographic elements that have shaped the area under study.

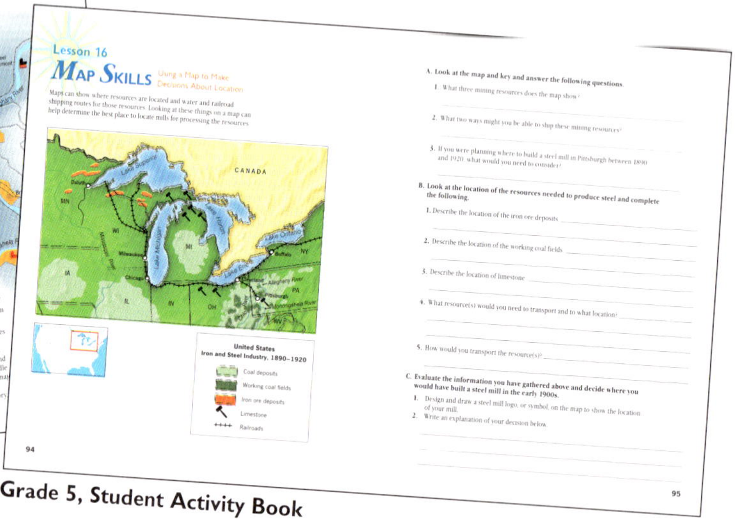

Grade 5, Student Activity Book

Two-page map skills lesson incorporates a map to further examine the area being explored in the lesson and features a list of questions to encourage students to use and strengthen their map skills.

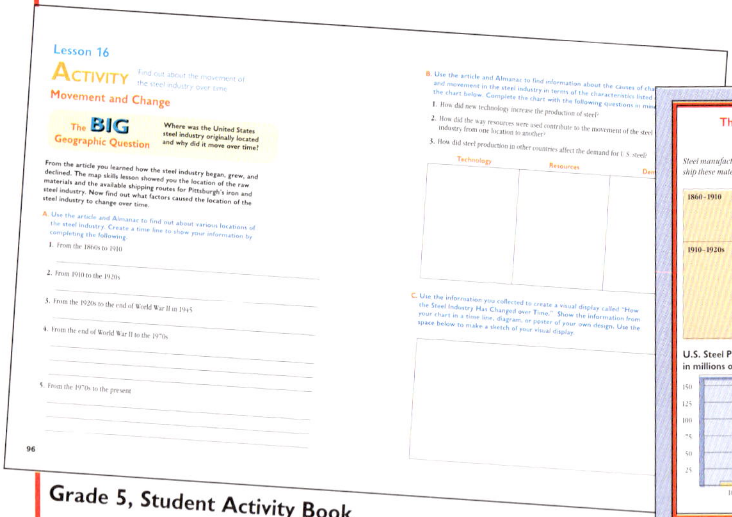

Grade 5, Student Activity Book

Two-page activity features a "Big Geographic Question" that requires students to use critical thinking skills to investigate a specific question and report their findings. These activity pages also feature a list of questions that require students to use the information they've learned in the lesson's informational article.

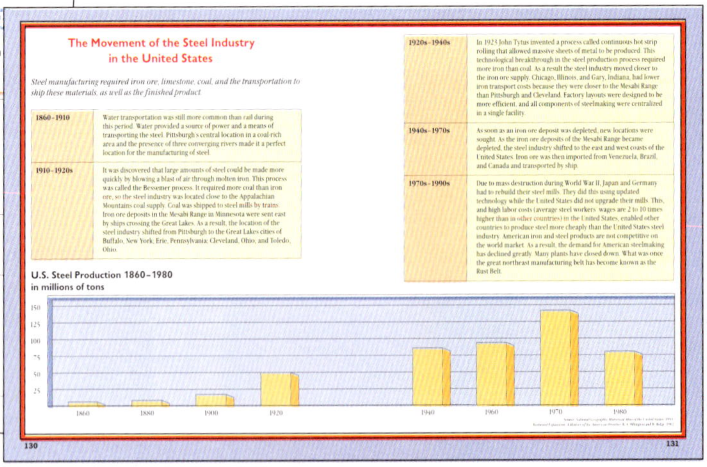

Grade 5, Student Activity Book

24-page Almanac of maps, charts, and data gives students an easy-to-access reference resource so they can locate information when they need it.

Now, teaching geography doesn't have to be an uphill battle.

We give you all the materials you need to cover the important territory effectively.

Cross-Curricular Connections tells you how other subject areas are integrated into each lesson.

Lesson Overview lets you set the stage for each lesson in one easy step.

Strategies for student activities help you take full advantage of the learning opportunities these activities provide.

Lesson Overview for pages 92–97: Students use written and graphic information to learn that steel mills were strategically located to minimize transportation costs.
Cross-Curricular Connection: Science – Understands the interactions between science, technology, and society; knows that science and technology have improved transportation, health, and communication

Lesson 16

Industry "STEEL" Remains

As you read about the steel industry, think about how geography has affected its growth, change, and movement.

Pittsburgh was a military outpost during the French and Indian War (1754–1763). In the mid-1800s it became the birthplace of the United States' steel-making industry. It sat upon a large coal deposit and near three rivers. Railways and the waterways of the Great Lakes gave the city access to the best iron ore deposits. This combination made steel production one of its early industries.

In Pittsburgh, the Allegheny and Monongahela rivers meet to form the Ohio River. The Ohio River provided a way to transport steel to markets across the country. As a result, the steel industry in the United States grew rapidly in the late 1800s.

Railroads were helping to open the West to settlers, and steel was needed for trains and rails. Also, the factories that had started the Industrial Revolution in the United States needed steel for tools and machines. Later, the auto industry used enormous amounts of steel as did the United States military in the two world wars. By the early 1900s Pittsburgh had become the nation's largest steel producer, with 34 steel plants lining its riverbanks.

A worker wears protective clothing for safety in one of Pittsburgh's steel mills.

92

National Geography Standards: 4, 14, 16
Basic Geography Skills: Acquiring and analyzing geographic information
Geographic Theme: Human/Environmental Interaction – Relationship within places

Informal Assessment: List the following events on the chalkboard and ask students to explain how they affected America's steel industry: the westward movement, the Industrial Revolution, the discovery of iron ore around Lake Superior, the invention of the Bessemer process, development of steel industries in other countries.

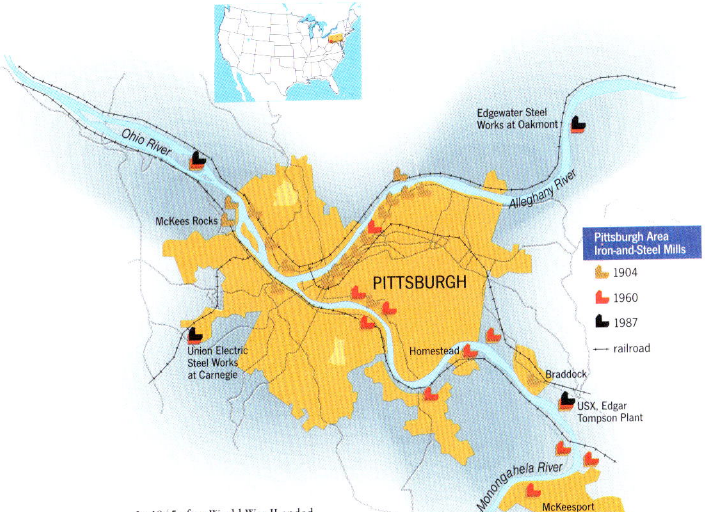

In 1945 after World War II ended, Japan and Germany began to rebuild their steel plants that had been destroyed during the war. Their plants were newer and more modern and efficient than those in the United States. They gave the United States steel industry stiff competition. As a result, United States and foreign companies began buying steel from other countries, where it was cheaper.

Today some countries that once bought steel from the United States now produce their own. The United States is no longer the world leader in steel production. The decline of steel mills in the United States has changed its industrial landscape. Far fewer railroads and factories are in use today. Land once occupied by mills now sits idle or is occupied by office buildings. Although Pittsburgh has new major industries, some steel is still produced there. The steel industry remains an important part of Pittsburgh's and our nation's history.

Program Resource: *National Geographic Picture Atlas of Our Fifty States*, pp. 56–57. Use to help students learn more about how Pennsylvania's physical features contributed to the growth of the state's iron and steel industry.
Learn More About It: *National Geographic Historical Atlas of the United States*, pp. 150–151

93

Grade 5, Teacher's Guide

Standards Correlations show you which geography standard, skill, or theme is being addressed in the current lesson, so you know you're covering the topics that matter the most.

Suggestions for classroom resources help you integrate each supplemental resource at a glance so you don't have to spend extra time planning.

Social Studies Concepts Scope and Sequence (Grades 3–6)

Grade 3: COMMUNITIES

Introduction to Geography
Lesson 1: *Our Planet Earth*
Lesson 2: *Your Place in Space*
Lesson 3: *Making a Map*

What Is A Community?
Lesson 4: *People Places*
Lesson 5: *It's a Plan!*
Lesson 6: *Four Fabulous Communities*

Our Earlier Communities
Lesson 7: *Adventure to the New World*
Lesson 8: *Our First Communities*
Lesson 9: *A Town Is Born: The Story of St. Augustine*

Types of Communities
Lesson 10: *Foods and Festivals*
Lesson 11: *A City Comes to Life*
Lesson 12: *The 'Burbs*

Community Connections
Lesson 13: *From Seed to Sandwich*
Lesson 14: *A Race for Life*
Lesson 15: *What's the Connection?*

Communities Change
Lesson 16: *From "Ghost Town" to "Ski Town"*
Lesson 17: *Houston's Horizon*
Lesson 18: *Islands of Fire and Rain*

Grade 4: REGIONS (States)

Introduction to Geography
Lesson 1: *Images of Earth*

Introduction to Regions
Lesson 2: *States United*
Lesson 3: *Time Changes Things*

New England
Lesson 4: *Land Changing Hands*
Lesson 5: *What's New in New England?*

The Middle Atlantic
Lesson 6: *From the Mountains to the Ocean*
Lesson 7: *BosWash MEGA What?*

The Southeast
Lesson 8: *Shrinking Swamps!*
Lesson 9: *From Cotton Belt to Sun Belt*

The Midwest
Lesson 10: *Heartland, USA!*
Lesson 11: *Dust Storm!*

The Southwest
Lesson 12: *A Southwestern Scrapbook*
Lesson 13: *A "Grand" Canyon*

The West
Lesson 14: *High and Dry*
Lesson 15: *The Diversity of California*
Lesson 16: *Timber!*

The Hawaiian Islands and Alaska
Lesson 17: *Island Treasures*
Lesson 18: *Journeying to Alaska*

When you have a lot of ground to cover, no other program does the job better.

Grade 5: UNITED STATES HISTORY

Introduction to Geography
Lesson 1: *Where on Earth?*
Lesson 2: *Getting a Map's Message*

The Land Prior to Columbus
Lesson 3: *Ever-Changing Earth*
Lesson 4: *Living off the Land*

The Age of Exploration
Lesson 5: *Tools for Traveling in Time*
Lesson 6: *Explore! Explore!*

The Colonial Period
Lesson 7: *Making a Living in a New Land*
Lesson 8: *Close Encounters*

The Revolution and Founding of a Nation
Lesson 9: *New York—A "Capital City"*
Lesson 10: *A Battle for Survival*

Westward Expansion
Lesson 11: *Westward Wagons*
Lesson 12: *Blazing the Western Trail*

The Civil War and Reconstruction
Lesson 13: *North vs. South*
Lesson 14: *Big City Bound*

Industrial Revolution
Lesson 15: *The Power of Waterfalls*
Lesson 16: *Industry "Steel" Remains*

The Twentieth Century
Lesson 17: *Frontiers of Technology*
Lesson 18: *Land of Opportunity*

Grade 6: WORLD HISTORY

Ancient Civilization
Lesson 1: *When the World Was Frozen*
Lesson 2: *Angry Waves*

Ancient Europe (Greece and Rome)
Lesson 3: *Onward, March!*
Lesson 4: *And the Winner Is . . .*

The Growth of Europe
Lesson 5: *Europe's Cities*
Lesson 6: *Europe's Rivers*

Eurasia
Lesson 7: *Two for One*
Lesson 8: *The Pearl of Siberia*

Middle East and North Africa
Lesson 9: *The World of Islam*
Lesson 10: *The Strait Story*

Africa South of the Sahara
Lesson 11: *Desert Diary*
Lesson 12: *A Fishy Story*

South Asia
Lesson 13: *Japan Closes Its Doors*
Lesson 14: *The Monsoon Season*

Southeast Asia, Oceania, and Australia
Lesson 15: *A Location Situation*
Lesson 16: *Diversity in the Pacific Islands*

North, South, and Central America
Lesson 17: *Defining Regions*
Lesson 18: *Connecting Oceans*

Map Skills Scope and Sequence (Grades 3–6)

Map Skills	Grade 3
Symbols (Interpreting dots, lines, colors, and symbols)	Lessons 6, 7, 8, 9, 10, 12, 13, 15, 17
Location (Using longitude, latitude, and/or grid systems to identify location)	Lessons 5, 14
Direction (Using cardinal and intermediate directions)	Lessons 4, 13, 14, 18
Scale (Figuring out distance or size)	Lesson 16
Construction (Making maps)	Lesson 2
Parts of Maps (Identifying the purpose of a map's title, main image, compass rose, legend, and scale)	Lessons 3, 8, 9, 10, 13, 15, 16, 17
Types of Maps (Identifying different types of maps)	Lessons 1, 7, 8, 9, 11, 13, 18
1. historical	Lessons 7, 9
2. physical	Lessons 1, 8, 11
3. political	Lesson 18
4. vegetation	
5. elevation and relief	
6. road	Lesson 13
7. population	Lesson 11

Map out a better approach to geography lessons.

Grade 4	Grade 5	Grade 6
Lessons 3, 4, 6, 9, 10, 11, 12, 13, 14, 16, 17, 18	Lessons 5, 7, 8, 9, 11, 12, 13, 14, 15, 16, 17, 18	Lessons 1, 2, 3, 4, 5, 7, 8, 9, 10, 11, 12, 13, 14, 16, 17
Lessons 7, 11	Lessons 3, 6, 10	Lessons 13, 16
Lessons 7, 9, 12, 14	Lessons 6, 10, 12	Lessons 6, 8, 11, 16
Lessons 14, 15	Lessons 5, 9, 11	Lessons 3, 5, 6, 8, 10, 11, 15, 18
Lessons 2, 8	Lesson 17	Lessons 9, 10, 18
Lessons 3, 4, 5, 6, 9, 10, 11, 12, 13, 16, 17, 18	Lessons 5, 7, 8, 9, 11, 12, 13, 14, 15, 16, 17, 18	Lessons 1, 2, 4, 5, 8, 9, 10, 11, 12, 13, 16, 17
Lessons 1, 2, 3, 4, 5, 6, 7, 8, 9, 14, 15, 16, 17, 18	Lessons 1, 2, 3, 4, 6, 7, 8, 9, 10, 11, 12, 13, 14, 15, 16	Lessons 1, 2, 3, 4, 5, 6, 7, 10, 11, 12, 13, 14, 15, 16, 17
Lessons 3, 4, 9, 14	Lessons 2, 4, 6, 7, 10, 12, 13, 14, 16	Lessons 3, 4
Lessons 1, 4, 5, 6, 7, 8, 15, 16	Lessons 1, 2, 3, 8, 11, 12	Lessons 2, 3, 4, 5, 6, 7, 8, 10, 11, 12, 13, 14
Lessons 2, 6, 7, 18	Lessons 2, 3, 9	Lessons 5, 10, 11, 12, 14, 15, 16
		Lessons 1, 14
Lesson 6	Lessons 8, 11, 15	Lessons 2, 5, 7, 14, 17
Lessons 7, 14		
Lessons 12, 17	Lessons 2, 4, 9, 14, 18	

National Geography Standards

STANDARDS	Lessons 1	2	3	4	5	6	7
I. THE WORLD IN SPATIAL TERMS							
1. Maps, globes, graphic tools for information in spatial perspective	🔴 🔵 🟢	🔴 🔵 🟢	🔴 🔵 🟢	🔵 🟢	🔵 🟢	🔵	🔵
2. Mental maps and spatial context		🔴 🔵 🟢	🟢	🟢			
3. Spatial organization of Earth	🔴 🔵 🟢	🔴 🔵 🟢	🔴 🔵 🟢	🔵 🟢	🔵 🟢		
II. PLACES AND REGIONS							
4. Physical and human characteristics of places	🔴	🟢	🟢	🔴 🟢	🔴	🔴 🔵 🟢	🔴 🔵 🟢
5. Regions interpret Earth's complexity							
6. Culture and experience change perception of places							
III. PHYSICAL SYSTEMS							
7. Physical processes shape Earth's surface						🔴	
8. Characteristics and distribution of Earth's ecosystems	🔵 🟢					🔵	
IV. HUMAN SYSTEMS							
9. Human populations							
10. Nature and complexity of Earth's cultural mosaics							
11. Patterns and networks of economic interdependence				🔴			
12. Human settlement					🔴 🟢		🔴 🔵 🟢
13. Forces of cooperation and conflict that shape Earth's surface				🔴			
V. ENVIRONMENT AND SOCIETY							
14. Human actions modify physical systems				🔴			
15. Physical systems affect human systems							
16. Meaning, distribution, and importance of resources				🔴		🟢	
VI. THE USES OF GEOGRAPHY							
17. How to apply geography to interpret the past					🔴		🔴 🔵 🟢
18. How to apply geography to interpret the present, and plan for the future							

🔴 in article 🔵 in map skills lesson 🟢 in activity

We've set a new standard for meeting the standards.

Lessons										
8	9	10	11	12	13	14	15	16	17	18
● blue	● blue	● blue	● blue		● blue ● green	● blue ● green	● blue	● blue	● blue ● green	● blue
				● blue						
				● red ● blue ● green				● blue	● green	● blue
● red ● blue ● green	● red ● green	● red ● blue				● red ● blue ● green		● red ● green		● red ● green
● red ● blue		● blue		● red		● red ● blue ● green				● green
		● green				● red ● green	● red ● green			● green
										● red ● green
									● blue	
			● green	● blue ● green						
			● red ● green							
● green			● red ● blue ● green	● red ● blue	● red ● blue ● green		● blue ● green		● red	
● red ● green	● red	● red	● red ● blue ● green					● red ● green		
	● green			● green	● red				● red ● blue ● green	
								● red	● red	● red
	● red ● blue ● green	● red ● blue ● green	● red	● red	● red ● blue ● green					
● red ● green	● blue			● green			● red ● blue ● green	● red ● green	● red	
● red							● red			

Geographic Themes

Organize your study of the world around the five geographic themes.

Lessons	THEMES LOCATION Position on Earth's surface	 PLACE Physical and human characteristics	 HUMAN/ ENVIRONMENTAL INTERACTION Relationship within places	 MOVEMENT Humans interacting on Earth	 REGIONS How they form and change
1		🔴 🔵 🟢			
2	🔴 🔵 🟢	🟢			
3	🔴 🟢	🔵 🟢			
4	🔵 🟢	🔴 🟢	🔴		
5	🔵	🔴 🟢			
6		🔴 🔵 🟢			
7		🔵		🔴 🟢	
8		🔴 🔵 🟢	🔴 🟢		🔵
9		🔴 🔵 🟢	🔴		
10	🔵		🔴 🔵 🟢		
11	🔵	🟢	🔴 🔵 🟢		
12		🔵	🟢	🔴 🔵 🟢	🔴
13	🔵 🟢			🔴 🔵 🟢	
14	🔵 🟢		🔴	🔴 🟢	
15				🔵 🟢	🔴
16	🔴 🔵	🟢			🟢
17	🔵 🟢	🔵 🟢	🔴		
18	🔵 🟢	🔴 🟢	🔴		

🔴 in article   🔵 in map skills lesson   🟢 in activity

Cross-Curricular Connections

Integrate geography into core curriculum areas.

Lessons	SUBJECT			
	Math	Science	History	Language Arts
1		🔴 🔵 🟢		
2	🔴 🔵			🟢
3	🔴 🔵			🟢
4			🔴 🔵	🟢
5	🔵		🔴 🟢	
6		🔴		🔵 🟢
7			🔴 🔵 🟢	
8			🔴 🔵 🟢	
9			🔴 🔵 🟢	
10			🔴	🔵 🟢
11	🔵		🔴	🟢
12			🔴 🔵	🟢
13		🔴 🟢	🔵	
14	🔵		🔴	🟢
15	🔵 🟢		🔴	
16	🔵		🔴 🟢	
17		🔴	🟢	🔵
18		🔴		🔵 🟢

🔴 in article 🔵 in map skills lesson 🟢 in activity

When it comes to understanding the world, you need to start at the bottom.

That's where all the secrets are hidden: the secrets to a country's prosperity, its character, its history, its future. All of the clues can be found at the bottom of it all, in a country's geographical structure.

SRA Geography

brings it to the surface with

Social Studies Integration. The 18 lessons included in each level of the program integrate with the topics most commonly addressed in grades 3–6 (communities, states and regions, United States history, and world history). This makes it easy for you to strengthen the geography strand of any social studies program.

Cross-Curricular Integration. Each level gives you the materials you need to integrate geography concepts with themes in history, language arts, math, and science.

Geography Standards and Guidelines. Each lesson addresses the themes, skills, standards, and essential elements set forth in the Geography for Life: National Standards 1994 that are now reflected in most state social studies guidelines.

Geography Skills and Understandings. Three-part lessons with geographic information, map skills, and critical thinking activities give students the opportunity to apply new skills immediately, so they can build their geographic understanding incrementally.

Multimedia Support. Supplemental materials created by the National Geographic Society include technology components to bring topics to life in a format that keeps students interested and involved.

Standardized Test Exposure. Each lesson includes an assessment that reflects the kinds of geographic questions students are asked on national and state tests.

SRA

GEOGRAPHY

Communities

AUTHORS
James F. Marran
Social Studies Chair Emeritus
New Trier Township High School
Winnetka, Illinois

Cathy L. Salter
Geography Teacher
Educational Consultant
Hartsburg, Missouri

SRA
McGraw-Hill
Columbus, Ohio

A Division of The ***McGraw·Hill*** *Companies*

Program Reviewers

Bonny Berryman
Eighth Grade Social Studies Teacher
Ramstad Middle School
Minot, North Dakota

Grace Foraker
Fourth Grade Teacher
B. B. Owen Elementary School
Lewisville Independent School District
Lewisville, Texas

Wendy M. Fries
Teacher/Visual and Performing Arts Specialist
Kings River Union School District
Tulare County, California

Maureen Maroney
Teacher
Horace Greeley I. S. 10 Queens
District 30
New York City, New York

Geraldeen Rude
Elementary Social Studies Teacher
1993 North Dakota Teacher of the Year
Minot Public Schools
Minot, North Dakota

Photo Credits

Cover, John Lawrence/Tony Stone Images; **2,** Paul Morrell/Tony Stone Images; **3,** (br) Aaron Haupt/SRA/McGraw-Hill; **8,** Ronnie Kaufman/The Stock Market; **9,** L.D. Gordon/ The Image Bank; **14,** Joseph H. Bailey/ National Geographic Image Collection; **20,** Corel Corporation; **21,** David W. Hamilton/The Image Bank; **26,** Patricia Lanza; **27,** David W. Hamilton/The Image Bank; **32,** (tr) Corel Corporation, (br) A.T. Willett/The Image Bank; **33,** (tr) Jeff Gnass/The Stock Market, (br) Pamela Zilly/The Image Bank; **38,** Archive Photos; **39,** (tr) North Wind Picture Archives, (br) John Henley/The Stock Market; **44,** The Image Bank; **45,** (tr) Randy Duchaine/ The Stock Market, (bl) Jean Anderson/The Stock Market; **46,** (tl)(t)(tc)(tr)(bl)(bc)(br) Corel Corporation; **50,** (b) Archive Photos; **51,** (t)(b) St. John's County Visitors and Convention Bureau; **62,** (t) Wes Thompson/The Stock Market, (br) David R. Frazier/Photo Researchers; **63,** (br) Eddie Hironaka/The Image Bank; **68,** Jack McConnell/ McConnell/McNamara; **69,** (tr) Randy Wells/Tony Stone Images, (bl) Russell D. Curtis/Photo Researchers, (br) David Pollack/The Stock Market; **74,** (bl) Alain Choisnet/The Image Bank, (tr) Peter Skinner/Photo Researchers, (br) John Kelly/The Image Bank; **75,** (bl) Alvis Upitis/The Image Bank, (rc) G. Covian/ The Image Bank, (tl) Randy O'Rourke/ The Stock Market; **80,** Fred Morris/The Stock Market; **86,** (bl) Lambert/Archive Photos, (tc)(br) Archive Photos, (tr) Kean/Archive Photos, (bc) Hirtz/Archive Photos; **87,** (tl)(tr)(br) Archive Photos, (bl) Corry/ Archive Photos; **92,** (bl) Geoff Juckes/The Stock Market, (c) Alan Becker/The Image Bank; **93,** (tr) Corel Corporation, (br) David Stoecklein/The Stock Market; **98-99,** Kunio Owaki/The Stock Market; **104,** (rc) Soames Summerhays/Photo Researchers; **105,** (tl) Gregory G.Dimijian/Photo Researchers; **124,** (t) Steve Elmore/The Stock Market, (c) Mark E. Gibson/ The Stock Market, (b) Audrey Gibson/The Stock Market.

SRA/McGraw-Hill
A Division of The ***McGraw-Hill*** *Companies*

Send all inquiries to:
SRA/McGraw-Hill
250 Old Wilson Bridge Road, Suite 310
Worthington, OH 43085

Printed in the United States of America.

ISBN 0-02-688161-6
2 3 4 5 6 7 8 9 POH 01 00 99 98 97

Table of Contents

Our Earlier Communities

Lesson 7

Lesson 8

Lesson 9

Types of Communities

Lesson 10

Lesson 11

Lesson 12

Community Connections

Communities Change

Lesson 1

OUR PLANET EARTH

As you read about Earth, think about two of its most important features—land and water.

From space, Earth looks like a big marble. Can you guess what the blue and brown patches are? If you guessed water and land, you are right! The blue patches are water. The brown patches are land. Some of the types of land features are plains, plateaus, hills, and mountains. But that's just the beginning! There's so much more to learn about our colorful planet.

Let's start with the patches of blue–water. You can probably name many types of bodies of water. Rivers, lakes, seas, and oceans are just a few. Here's an amazing fact: nearly three fourths of Earth's surface is covered by water, but only a very small portion of that water is drinkable. Most of Earth's water is salty.

The water that surrounds the land on Earth is divided into four huge areas called oceans. They are the Pacific, Atlantic, Indian, and Arctic oceans. The largest and deepest ocean is the Pacific Ocean. **Geographers,** people who study Earth's surface, have found that the Pacific Ocean covers about one third of Earth's surface.

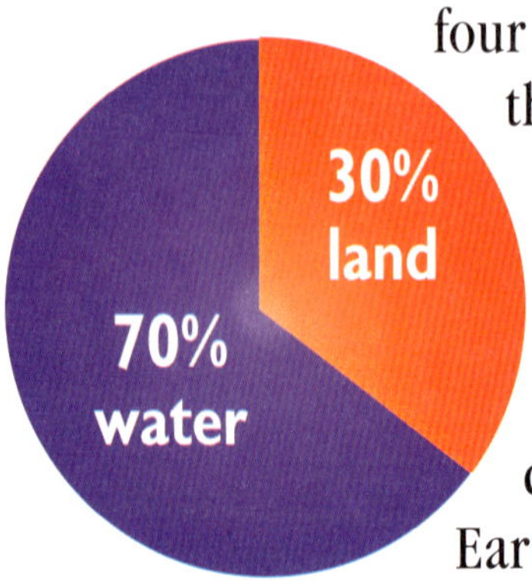

National Geography Standards: 1, 3, 4
Basic Geography Skills: Acquiring and analyzing geographic information
Geographic Theme: Place – Physical and human characteristics

Informal Assessment: Have students demonstrate their understanding by identifying the continent where they live and the bodies of water that surround it.

Let's move on to the brown patches–land. The land on Earth's surface is divided into several big pieces called **continents.** There are seven continents.

Look at the map below. See how many oceans and continents you can locate and name. Can you find all four oceans and all seven continents?

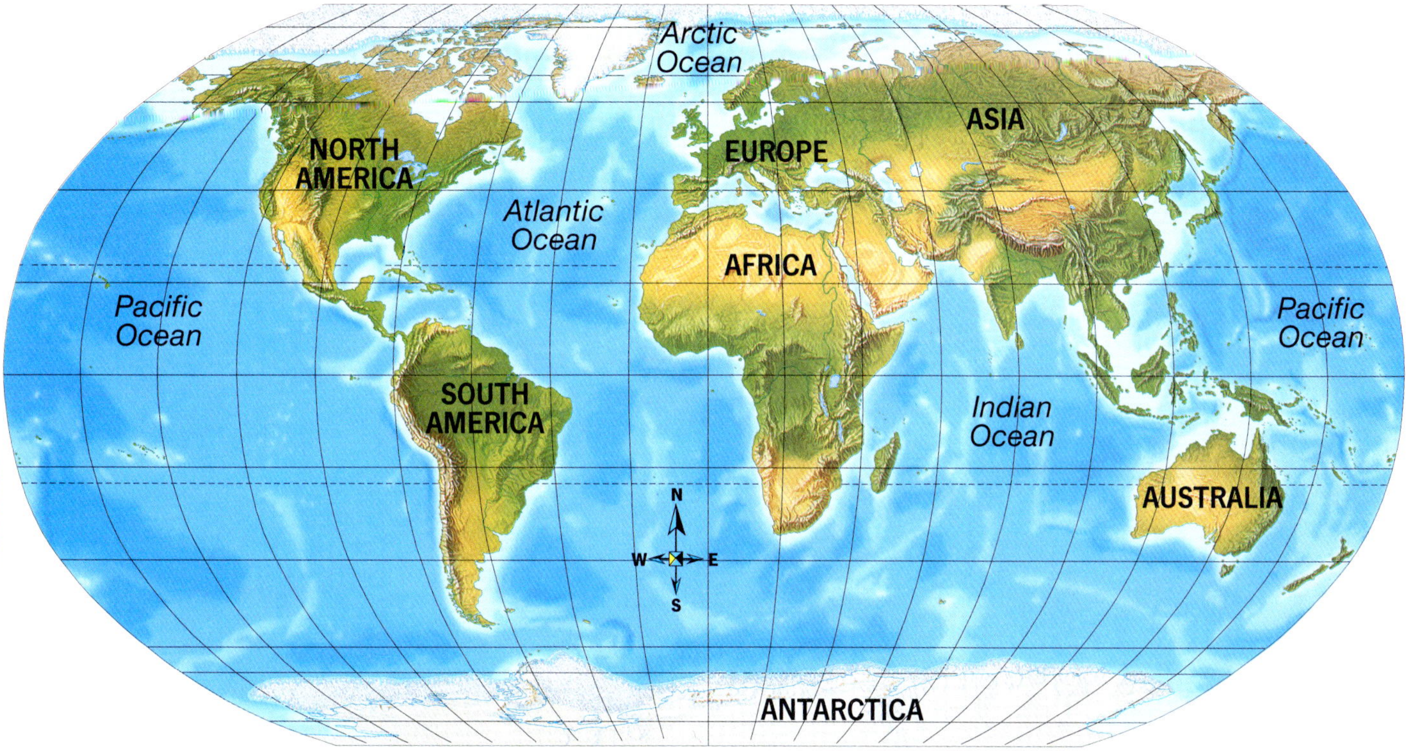

This world map of Earth's surface shows its physical features such as oceans and continents. The map is drawn on a flat surface.

A globe also shows the physical features of Earth, but it has a different shape. It is round like Earth. What continents and oceans can you see on this globe?

Program Resource: *National Geographic CD-ROM: Picture Atlas of the World.* Use to view the different land and water features of Earth.

Map Skills Objective: Learn names, definitions, locations, and appearances of different forms of land and water on Earth.
Cross-Curricular Connection: Science – Understands basic features of Earth; knows that Earth material consists of solid land and liquid water

Lesson 1
MAP SKILLS
Using a Physical Map to Learn about Land and Water

Two of Earth's most important physical features are land and water. This **physical map** shows some of the landforms and water forms.

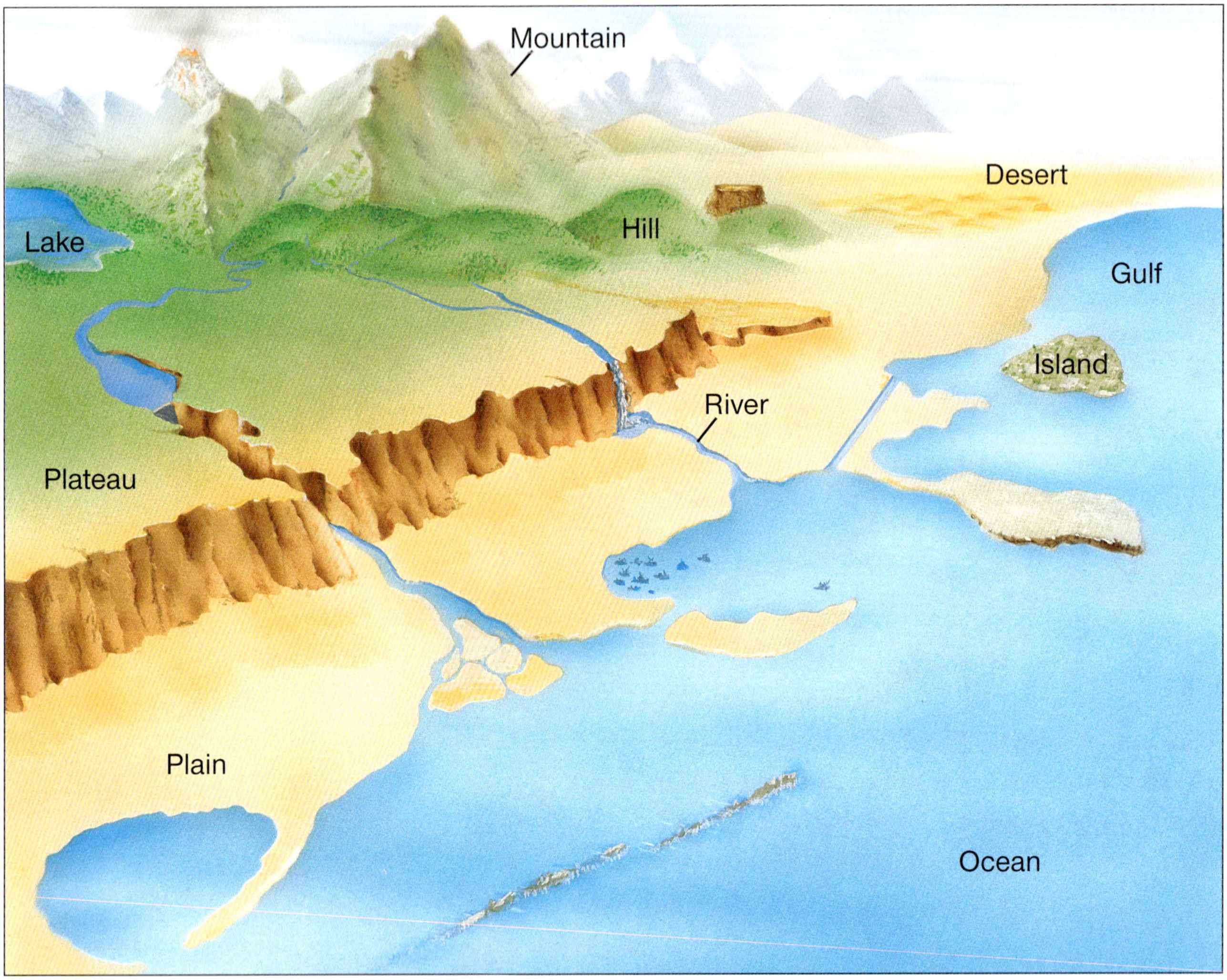

desert – a large, dry area of land with little or no rainfall

gulf – an area of ocean or sea partially surrounded by curved land

hill – a raised piece of land that is smaller than a mountain

island – a piece of land surrounded by water on all sides

lake – a body of water smaller than an ocean and surrounded by land

mountain – peaked land that rises very high above the land around it

ocean – a huge body of salt water that covers nearly three fourths of Earth's surface

plain – a large area of flat or gently rolling land

plateau – a large, flat area of land that rises higher than the land around it

river – a large stream of water that flows through land

National Geography Standards: 1, 3, 8
Basic Geography Skills: Acquiring, analyzing, and organizing geographic information
Geographic Theme: Place – Physical and human characteristics

Informal Assessment: Check to make sure students have correctly identified each physical feature as a landform or water form. Have them explain any incorrect answer.

1. Study the map. Read each word and its definition.
   How many kinds of landforms and water forms are shown on the map? 10

2. Find the word ***mountain*** on the physical map.
   Is a mountain a landform or a water form? If it is a landform,
   write the letter ***L*** above the word on the map.
   If it is a water form, write the letter ***W*** above the word on the map.

3. Find the word ***river*** on the physical map.
   Is a river a landform or a water form? If it is a landform,
   write ***L*** above the word. If it is a water form, write ***W*** above the word.

4. Write ***L*** or ***W*** above each of the other eight forms of land and water shown on the map.

5. Using the information you recorded on the map, list each land and water feature in the correct column below.

Land	Water
desert	gulf
hill	lake
island	ocean
mountain	river
plain	
plateau	

Activity Objective: Learn the names and definitions of different forms of land and water.
Cross-Curricular Connection: Science — Understands basic features of Earth; knows that Earth material consists of solid land and liquid water
Almanac: See page 110.

Lesson 1

ACTIVITY Create a game to learn forms of land and water.

A Geography Game

The BIG Geographic Question What are the different forms of land and water?

From the article you learned that land and water are the two main physical features of Earth. The map skills lesson showed you some of the different forms of land and water. Now create a game to help you and your classmates learn the names of the different forms of land and water.

A. Remind yourself of the main bodies of land and water on Earth.

1. List the seven continents below.

a. Africa
b. Antarctica
c. Asia
d. Australia
e. Europe
f. North America
g. South America

2. List the four oceans below.

a. Atlantic
b. Arctic
c. Indian
d. Pacific

National Geography Standards: 1, 3, 8
Basic Geography Skills: Organizing geographic information and answering geographic questions
Geographic Theme: Place — Physical and human characteristics

Informal Assessment: After groups share their games, have the class discuss how the games helped them to learn and remember the different forms of land and water on Earth.
Standardized Test-Format Assessment: See page 147.

B. Look back at the different forms of land and water shown on pages 4–5.

1. List the landforms below.

a. desert
b. hill
c. island
d. mountain
e. plain
f. plateau

2. List the water forms below.

a. gulf
b. lake
c. ocean
d. river

C. Write down the names of some of your favorite games. What game could you make to help you learn the names of oceans, continents, landforms, and water forms?

Bingo
Go Fish
Concentration
Jeopardy

D. Think about how you will teach the game to your classmates. Write simple directions for playing your game on the lines below.

(Make sure students' directions clearly explain how to play their games.)

E. Make your game. First, try it out with a family member or friend to see if you need to make any changes. Make the changes, then teach your game to a classmate. (You may wish to invite students to teach their games to each other in small groups or in front of the class.)

Materials: posterboard, paper, construction paper, markers, crayons, scissors, glue

Lesson Overview for pages 8–13: Students use written and graphic information to understand the concept of "place in space" in varying scales.
Cross-Curricular Connection: Math – Recognizes the relationship between size and scale

Lesson 2

Your Place in Space

As you read about your place in space, think about how you might represent the many places in which you live.

What place do you have in the space of your family?

How do you answer when someone asks you where you live? There are many ways to answer this question.

The first thing you might think of is your home. At home, you have a place in the space of your family. You are a brother or sister, a son or daughter. Your family lives in a home. You may think about the rooms in your home. Your home is one of your places in space.

Next you may think about the street where your home is located. That street is part of a community. Maybe a picture of your neighborhood street comes into your mind. Or maybe a picture of you and your family walking in a community park enters your mind. Your community is another one of your places in space.

Look for your community on a city or state map. You may or may not find it there by name, but you will probably find a nearby city that you recognize. Circle or write in your community's name on the map if it isn't already there. The city in which your community is located or near your community is another one of your places in space.

National Geography Standards: 1, 2, 3
Basic Geography Skills: Asking and answering geographic questions; organizing geographic information
Geographic Theme: Location – Position on Earth's surface

Informal Assessment: Ask students which is bigger — a community or a state, a state or the United States, the United States or the world. Then ask them which of these places fits inside each other.

While looking at the city map, you may notice the state in which the city and your community are located. The state in which you live is another one of your places in space. If you looked at a United States map, you would find your state on it. If you looked at a world map, you would find the United States on it. And if you looked at a map of the solar system, you would find the world, or Earth, on it!

Look at the **mental map,** a way of organizing information in your mind, below. It is one way of thinking about your place in space. Find another example of a mental map in the Almanac in the back of the book.

Yes! Your family, your home, your community, your city, your state, the United States, North America, and Earth are all your "place in space." The picture in your mind of your place in space may have started out small, but it got bigger and bigger! When someone asks you where you live, how will you answer? You'll probably just give your address. But, in your mind, you can picture a lot more.

You have a special place in the world.

A mental map that represents your place in space, might look like this.

Program Resource: *National Geographic CD-ROM: Picture Atlas of the World.* Use to locate one's state, country, and continent.

Lesson 2
MAP SKILLS Making Mental Maps

Mental maps are our ideas of where something is and how to get to it. They are images we store in our minds. When we can't get our hands on a real map, mental maps help us remember how to get to what we want or where we want to go. Sunbury is a small community located near the bigger city of Columbus, Ohio. Use this map of Sunbury to practice making a mental map.

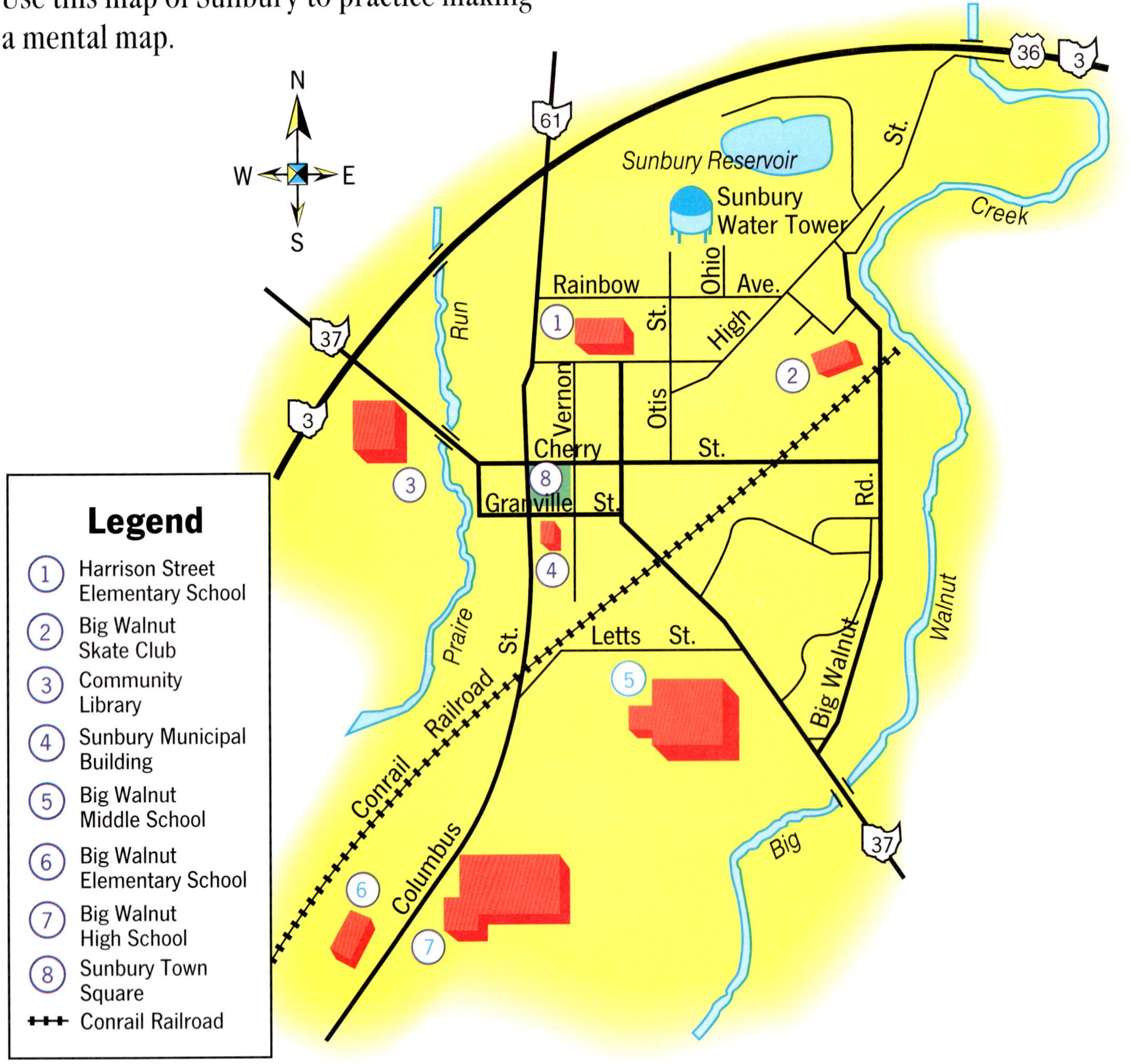

National Geography Standards: 1, 2, 3
Basic Geography Skills: Asking and answering geographic questions; organizing and analyzing geographic information
Geographic Theme: Location — Position on Earth's surface

Informal Assessment: Check students' understanding of mental maps by having them discuss how they were able to remember where some of the places were located on the Sunbury map. For instance, they could have remembered the town square because it was shaped like a square or they remembered seeing it towards the center of town.

1. Where is the town square located?

in the center of town or just west of the center of town

2. Write the names of the four streets that surround the town square.

Cherry Street — Granville Street

Columbus Street — Vernon Street

3. Which two of the four streets listed above run north and south?

Columbus and Vernon Streets

4. Which two of the four streets listed above run east and west?

Granville and Cherry Streets

5. List the names of some interesting places in Sunbury and where they are located.

Place Name	Location
Community Library	west of the town square
Sunbury Water Tower	north of town square, near Sunbury Reservoir
Big Walnut Skate Club	north of Cherry Street, near railroad tracks
Big Walnut Elementary School	on Columbus Street, south of the town square
Big Walnut Creek	runs north and south along the east side of town

6. Now cover up the map of Sunbury with a piece of paper. Try to remember what it looked like. Draw a picture of it in your mind. Using your mental map and your notes from questions 3, 4, and 5 above, draw a map of Sunbury on paper. When you are finished, uncover the map in your book and compare it to the one you drew. How accurate was your mental map?

(Check students' maps drawn from memory for similarities to the Sunbury map.)

Activity Objective: Determine one's own place in space.
Cross-Curricular Connection: Language Arts — Effectively gathers/uses information for research; asks and seeks to answer questions regarding the characteristics of people and places in one's local community
Almanac: See pages 112–113, 116–117, and 128.

Lesson 2

ACTIVITY Make a mental map of your own "place in space."

Your Place, Your Space

The BIG Geographic Question — **Where do you live?**

In the article you learned about the many places that you can say you live. The map skills lesson gave you some practice in making a mental map. Now you will make a mental map of your place in space to show the many places you live.

A. A mental map can be of a big or small space. It can be specific or general.

1. Write the name of your community or town.

(Students should provide answers specific to their place.)

2. List some of the land and water features, buildings, and fun places to go in your community. (Make sure the places and features students list are in or likely to be in their communities.)

Land Features	Water Features	Buildings	Fun Places to Go

National Geography Standards: 1, 2, 3, 4
Basic Geography Skills: Asking and answering geographic questions; acquiring, organizing, and analyzing geographic information
Geographic Themes: Location — Position on Earth's surface; Place — Physical and human characteristics

Informal Assessment: Have students orally tell their place in space, going from either largest space (Earth) to smallest, or from smallest (family unit or home) to largest.
Standardized Test-Format Assessment: See page 148.

3. Think about the features you listed in the chart and what your community or town looks like.
4. Draw a mental map of your community or town like you did for Sunbury.

B. Think about the bigger, more general areas that include your community or town. To help you with this, answer the following questions.

(Check students' answers and mental maps to see whether they show an understanding of the various places in space that they occupy—home, community, city, state, U.S., North America, and world—in terms of scale.)

1. Near what bigger city is your community or town located?

____

2. In what state is your community or town located?

____

3. Use the United States map in the Almanac to locate your state.
4. Use the world map in the Almanac to locate the United States.

C. The "bull's-eye" mental map that you saw on page 9 is one way to show your place in space. Look in the Almanac for an example of a mental map for a person who lives in Atlanta. Now create a mental map that shows your place in the bigger space of the world.

Lesson Overview for pages 14–19: Use written and graphic information to understand how to use different maps to convey different kinds of information.
Cross-Curricular Connection: Math – Understands general nature/uses of mathematics; understands that mathematical ideas/concepts can be represented concretely, graphically, and symbolically

Lesson 3

Making a MAP

As you read about the features or elements of a map, think about a map you'd like to make and share.

A **map** is a flat drawing that represents a place. It shows a bird's-eye view of parts of our world. Some maps are very simple; others are detailed. Either way, maps are important tools for providing information.

When planning a map, a mapmaker must decide two things: what the map will be about and what features are important to show and explain. The most important thing is this–it must be easy to understand!

A **map's scale** helps us figure out how far from each other places on a map really are. The scale may show that one inch on the map equals 10 miles on the ground.

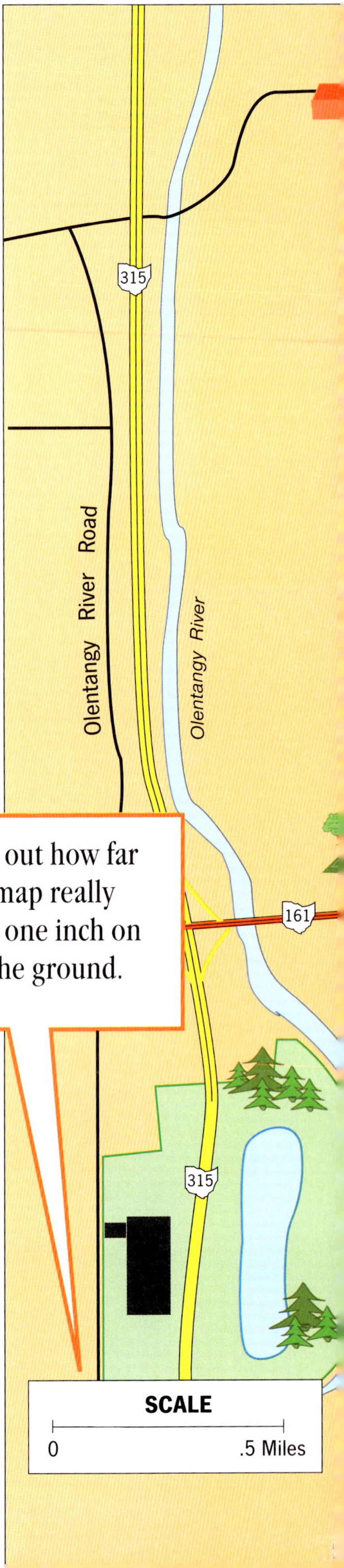

Did you know that the making and study of maps is cartography? Someone who draws maps is called a **cartographer.**

National Geography Standards: 1, 3
Basic Geography Skill: Acquiring geographic information
Geographic Theme: Location – Position on Earth's surface

Informal Assessment: Have an assortment of maps available for groups of students to study. Have students identify the main parts of the maps as described in the lesson. Discuss any other interesting features students find on the maps.

A map's main image is the map itself. This map of Old Worthington shows some of the things you might see in a neighborhood, such as bodies of water, buildings, streets, and railroads.

The **title** tells you what the map is showing.

A **compass rose** shows direction. The four main, or **cardinal**, directions are north, south, east, and west.

A map's **legend**, or key, lists and explains each symbol and color used on a map. Symbols save space. They make maps less crowded and easier to read.

Learn More About It: *National Geographic: Exploring Your World,* pp. 324–333

Map Skills Objective: Use different kinds of maps to get different information.
Cross-Curricular Connection: Math — Understands that mathematical ideas/concepts can be represented concretely, graphically, and symbolically

Lesson 3
MAP SKILLS Using Maps to Get Information

Different maps show different information. A map can show the layout of a building or how many people live in a city. It can also show us how to get to a place or where to have fun.

Map A

Sturgeon Elementary School, 1975
Lawrenceville, VA
(Floor Plan)

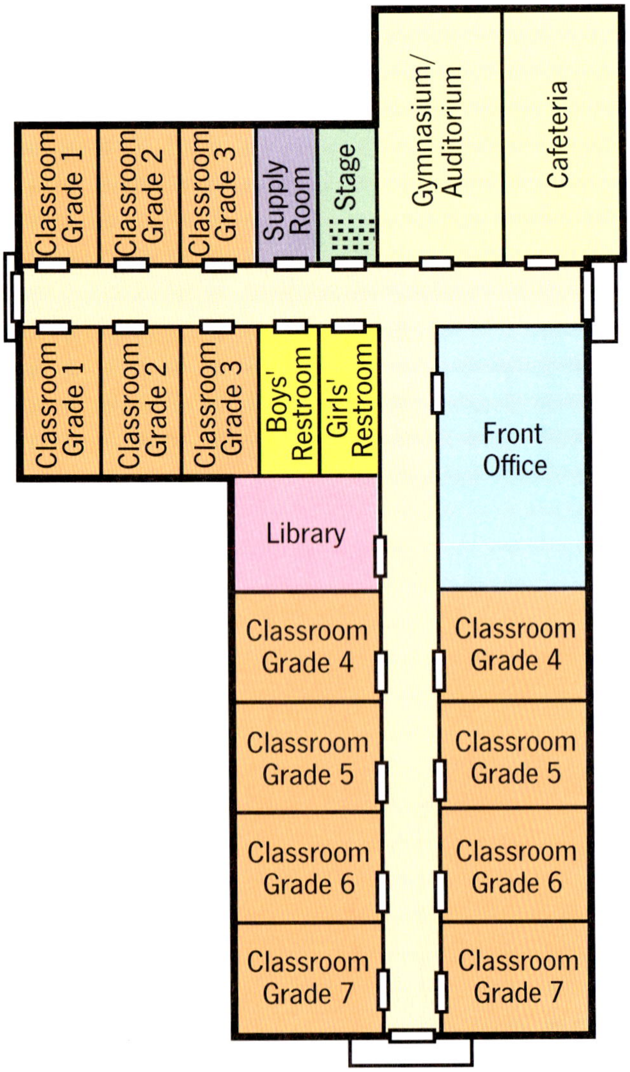

Map B

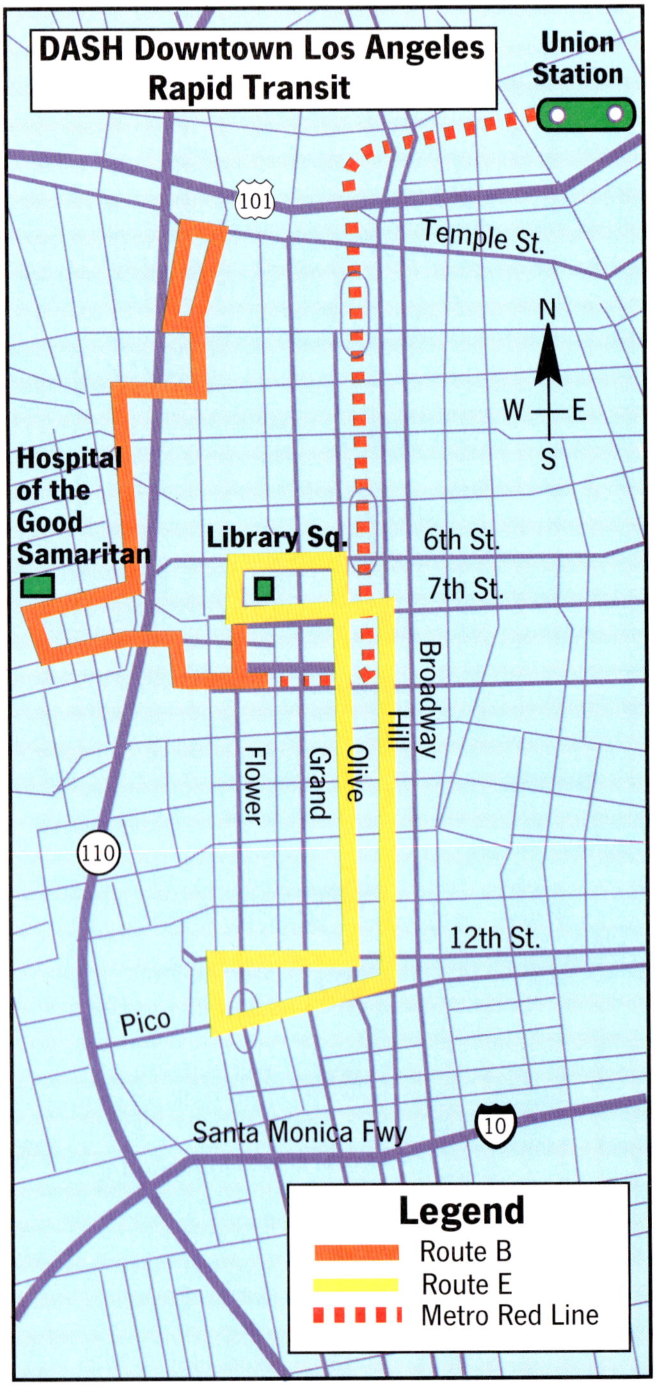

National Geography Standards: 1, 3
Basic Geography Skills: Acquiring and analyzing geographic information
Geographic Theme: Place — Physical and human characteristics

Informal Assessment: Write just the titles of different kinds of maps (school, transportation, population, recreation, and so on) on the board, and ask students which one they would use to find certain information (for example, Which map shows how many people live in an area? Which shows how to get to a certain classroom? Which shows where to ride a bike? and so on).

A. Look at Maps A and B.

1. Which map tells you which bus to take to Library Square?

   Map B

2. Which map can help visitors find their way around an elementary school?

   Map A

B. Answer these questions about Map A.

1. What is the title of Map A? Sturgeon Elementary School, 1975
2. Does the school have a gym? Yes
3. Draw a line to show how to go from the library to the supply room.
   (Students should draw a direct route using hallways from library to the supply room.)
4. Write one sentence describing the information this map gives.

   It shows where different rooms are located in the Sturgeon Elementary School.

5. What do you think this map can be used for?

   It could be used by new students and visitors to find their way around.

C. Answer these questions about Map B.

1. What is the title of Map B? DASH Downtown Los Angeles Rapid Transit
2. Which bus route takes you to Library Square? Route E
3. Where does the Metro Red Line take you?

   Union Station or downtown from Union Station

4. Write one sentence describing the information this map gives.

   It shows how to get to different places by bus or Metro Red Line in downtown Los Angeles.

5. What do you think this map can be used for?

   It could be used to help tourists find their way around the city by bus or Metro Red Line.

Activity Objective: Make a map that effectively provides information and communicates a message.
Cross-Curricular Connection: Language Arts — Effectively gathers/uses information for research; presents information obtained from research in a display that integrates multiple representations of information
Almanac: See page 129.

Lesson 3

ACTIVITY

Make a map that provides information and communicates a message.

Mapping a Message

The BIG Geographic Question

How do maps communicate information?

From the article you learned some of the basic features of a map and their purposes. The map skills lesson showed you that different kinds of maps are used to communicate different kinds of information. Now create a map that communicates information to a family member or friend.

A. Read the below list of different types of maps. Circle the type of map that you think you would like to create. You may want to look in the Almanac for examples of other types of maps, such as a recreation or population map. Or you can add your own ideas to the list below. (Make sure students select a type of map to create.)

a map of how to get to your room in your house

a neighborhood street map

a map of your school bus route

a map of the land and water features of a nearby park

a map of where you hid something last year

____

____

____

____

National Geography Standards: 1, 2, 3, 4
Basic Geography Skills: Acquiring, organizing, and analyzing geographic information
Geographic Themes: Location — Position on Earth's surface; Place — Physical and human characteristics

Informal Assessment: Group students according to the types of maps they made. Have students tell how their maps are alike and different. Help them see that even maps about a similar topic can be different in many ways. Have them discuss why some maps are easier to understand than others.
Standardized Test-Format Assessment: See page 149.

B. Make a list of things to include on your map. Look back at the article on pages 14 and 15 for suggestions. (Make sure students list key map elements.)

______________________ ______________________

______________________ ______________________

______________________ ______________________

C. Think about your map's legend. Choose four things on your map that you could show as symbols. Write one of the names in the space at the top of each box. Then draw the symbols in the larger boxes. (Make sure students' symbols and names match and are clear.)

D. Make a practice sketch of your map so you can plan where to put everything. (Check students' sketches for necessary map elements.)

E. Make a final version of your map. Have a family member, friend, or classmate read your map and describe the information or message shown. Was their answer correct? Did your map communicate the message you wanted? If not, how could you change it to make it more clear? (You may wish to have students compare their maps.)

Lesson Overview for pages 20–25: Students use written and graphic materials depicting various community interactions to understand what comprises a community.
Cross-Curricular Connection: History — Understands how communities in North America varied long ago; knows the geographical settings, economic activities, food, clothing, homes, crafts, and rituals of Native American societies long ago

Lesson 4

People Places

As you read about the town of Petersburg, think about the different people and places that make up a community.

Community services help everyone. How do they help children?

Petersburg is a suburban community near Richmond, the capital city of Virginia. A long time ago, it was an important battle site during the Civil War of 1861–1865. During that time Petersburg was mostly farmland where tobacco was grown. Now there are more houses than fields in Petersburg, but farming is still important to the community.

Today Petersburg is a spread-out surburban community. A lot of people there live in subdivisions, or areas of land divided into lots for building houses. Many of the subdivisions have recycling programs. This means that the community members are finding ways to reuse things instead of throwing them away.

The Petersburg community has post offices, libraries, hospitals, police and fire stations, federal government offices, and other services. There are several schools in Petersburg. The town has also just built a shopping mall near the interstate highway. This location makes the mall easy to get to by people who live in Petersburg and people traveling through the area.

National Geography Standards: 4, 11, 14, 16
Basic Geography Skill: Acquiring geographic information
Geographic Themes: Human/Environmental Interaction — Relationship within places; Place — Physical and human characteristics

Informal Assessment: Help students complete a chart showing how people and places interact in a community. For example:

People with People:	services like buses	projects like recycling	celebrations
People with Places:	using the water to move goods	boating, fishing	going to school

Many of the people who live in Petersburg have jobs downtown. They work in stores and offices. Other people who live in Petersburg go to jobs in the city of Richmond, less than 30 minutes away. Some of them take the bus to work every morning, and some of them drive.

On the edge of town is the Appomattox River. Long ago plantation owners used the river to travel and to send and receive goods. Today businesses use the river to ship goods to and receive goods from other cities. The people of Petersburg enjoy boating and fishing on the river.

The people of Petersburg work together and play together. They depend on each other for goods and services and to have fun. They know that a community is a place, but it is people, too.

These boys and girls are on their way to school. Do you ride a bus to school?

Program Resource: *National Geographic Picture Atlas of Our World*, p. 21; *National Geographic Software: Zip Zap Map! USA.* Use to help students become familiar with using a map legend.
Learn More About It: *National Geographic: Exploring Your World*, p. 124

Map Skills Objective: Use cardinal and intermediate directions to locate places on a map.
Cross-Curricular Connection: History — Understands how communities in North America varied long ago; knows the geographical settings, economic activities, food, clothing, homes, crafts, and rituals of Native American societies long ago

Lesson 4

MAP SKILLS Using a Map Compass

If you were a visitor in Petersburg, a map could help you find your way around. Many maps have a symbol called a compass or compass rose that shows the four cardinal directions–north, south, east, and west.

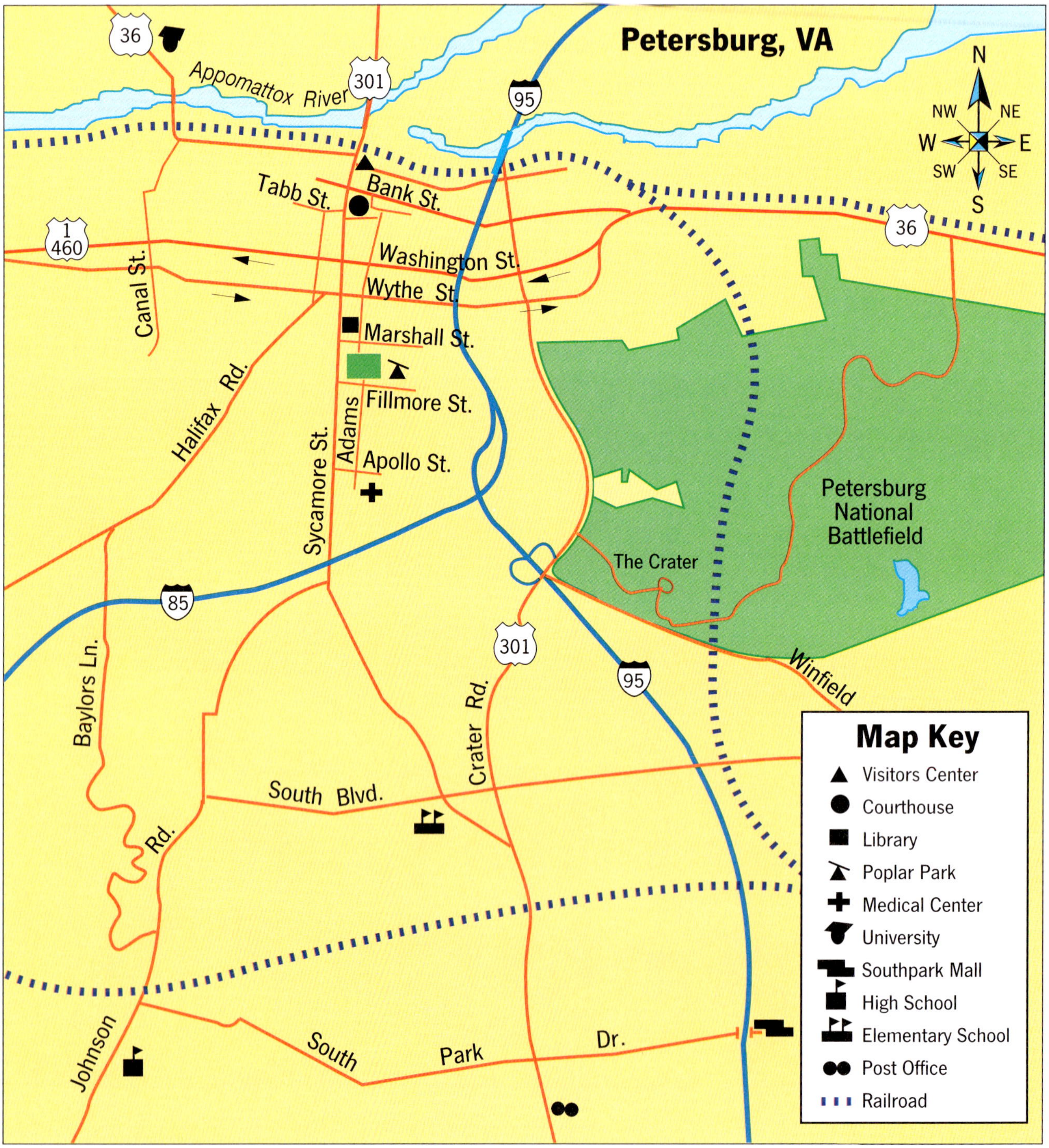

National Geography Standards: 1, 3
Basic Geography Skills: Analyzing geographic information and answering geographic questions
Geographic Theme: Location — Position on Earth's surface

Informal Assessment: Starting from a central point on the map, check students' cardinal and intermediate directions. Then check their ability to use directions to find a route from one point to another.

A. If you were at Petersburg National Battlefield, which direction would you go to get to these places?

1. medical center west
2. post office south
3. visitors center north; northwest

Northeast is an **intermediate direction**—a direction halfway between two cardinal directions. The other intermediate directions are northwest, southeast, and southwest.

4. In which direction would you travel from the battlefield to the Appomattox River? northwest
5. In which direction would you go from the Medical Center to Southpark Mall? southeast

B. Follow these directions. Where are you?

1. Start at the high school. Go north on Johnson Rd. to Sycamore St. Go south on Sycamore St. to South Blvd.

   the elementary school

2. Start at the post office. Go north on Crater Rd. to Washington St. Go west on Washington St. to Sycamore St. Go south on Sycamore St. Stop at the corner of Marshall St.

   the library

C. Now that you can find your way around Petersburg, you can give directions to someone else.

1. Tell how to get from the high school to Poplar Park.

   north on Johnson Rd., north on Sycamore St., east on Fillmore St.

2. Tell how to get from the Courthouse to Southpark Mall.

   south on Sycamore St., south on Crater Rd., east on South Park Dr.

Activity Objective: Find a place in one's community and map a route to get to a place in the community.
Cross-Curricular Connection: Language Arts — Demonstrates competence in the general skills/strategies of the writing process
Almanac: See page 127.

Lesson 4

ACTIVITY

Use a map to show how to find a place in your community.

Where Are You?

The BIG Geographic Question

How can you help visitors find their way around your community?

In the article you read about some of the people and places in the community of Petersburg. The map skills lesson helped you find your way to some of the important places. Now use what you know about directions to make a map of your community.

A. Make a list of important places in your community. An example has been done for you. (Make sure the places students list are in their community.)

1. school
2. ____________________
3. ____________________
4. ____________________

B. Think of symbols to stand for the places on your map. Draw a symbol in each box. (Map key symbols should be appropriate.)

1.

2.

National Geography Standards: 1, 2, 3, 4
Basic Geography Skills: Asking geographic questions and organizing geographic information
Geographic Themes: Location — Position on Earth's surface; Place — Physical and human characteristics

Informal Assessment: Have students who have given directions to the same place compare their maps and directions. Encourage them to help one another clarify their directions.
Standardized Test-Format Assessment: See page 150.

3.

4.

C. List at least five streets that will be on your map.

1. (Students should list streets near the places they named in A.) ______
2. ______
3. ______
4. ______
5. ______

D. Draw a map of your community. Be sure your map includes all the places and streets from your lists. Also include a map key.

(Check to see whether students' maps accurately indicate places in the community.)

E. Write directions.

1. Choose one of the places on your map. Draw the way to go from your school to that place. (Make sure students have drawn a route on their maps.)
2. Write directions from your school to that place. Be sure to include street names and compass directions. (Make sure students' directions are accurate according to their maps.)

______

______

______

Lesson Overview for pages 26–31: Students use written and graphic information about Washington, D.C., as a model for understanding a planned community.
Cross-Curricular Connection: History – Understands national symbols through which American values/principles are expressed

Lesson 5

It's a PLAN!

As you read about the plan for Washington, D.C., think about how geography affected where the city is and how it was designed.

The year was 1790. The United States did not have a permanent capital. Instead, the government had moved eight times from one city to another. Finally the nation's leaders decided the government should have a permanent home. But where?

L'Enfant's plan made the Capitol building the center of the city.

President George Washington was asked to choose the site for the nation's new capital. In 1791 he picked a location between the states of Maryland and Virginia. The decision to place the capital on the Potomac River was based on geography. Washington believed that the location would provide a good port. The new capital would also be centrally located in the nation.

Pierre-Charles L'Enfant, a young French engineer, was chosen to plan the capital. L'Enfant believed in the United States' future. He had grand ideas for the new capital.

In fact, some of L'Enfant's ideas were too grand. But he would not compromise, or give up any of his plans in order to reach an agreement. In 1792 President Washington dismissed L'Enfant and found someone else to plan the capital city.

National Geography Standards: 4, 12, 17
Basic Geography Skill: Analyzing geographic information
Geographic Theme: Place – Physical and human characteristics

Informal Assessment: Have students complete a time line sequencing the planning of Washington, D.C.

1790	1791	1791	1792	1800
The nation's leaders decide to build a permanent capital.	President Washington selects the site.	L'Enfant is chosen to plan the new capital.	L'Enfant is replaced by Ellicott and Banneker.	Congress meets in the half-finished capital.

Andrew Ellicott and Benjamin Banneker were the new planners. Using parts of L'Enfant's original plan, they put the Capitol, the building where Congress meets, in the center of the city.

Ellicott and Banneker laid out the streets in a **grid** pattern to make the city easy to travel across. A grid is a system of lines that forms boxes. The streets that ran east and west were named with letters. The streets that ran north and south were named with numbers. Diagonal streets were named for states of the union. Many streets met in the middle of the city in hubs, or circles.

In 1800 the government moved to its new home. A well-organized street plan and a central location near a major waterway made it a true "capital" city!

L'Enfant's plans included the Mall, a broad, green park lined with many important buildings. One of them is the Washington Monument.

Program Resource: *National Geographic Picture Atlas of Our Fifty States*, pp. 20–23; *National Geographic Software: Zip Zap Map! USA*. Use to help students learn more about the growth and buildings of Washington, D.C.

Map Skills Objective: Use the grid system to locate streets and places on a community map.
Cross-Curricular Connection: Math — Understands/applies concepts of geometry

Lesson 5

MAP SKILLS Using a Grid to Locate Places

Using a map grid can help you find places on a map easily. Look at the map of Washington, D.C., below. Suppose you want to find the Capitol building. First, you look for the word ***Capitol*** in the Map Index. Next to ***Capitol*** in the index, it says E17.

To find grid box E17, find the letter ***E*** along one side of the map. Then move your other finger across the top or bottom of the map until it is under the number ***17.*** The box where ***E*** meets ***17*** is where you will find the Capitol building.

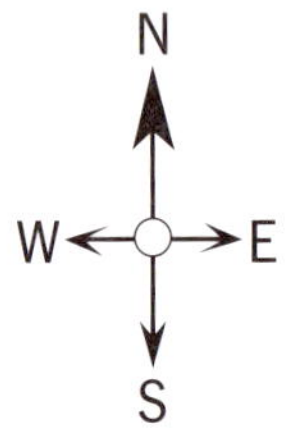

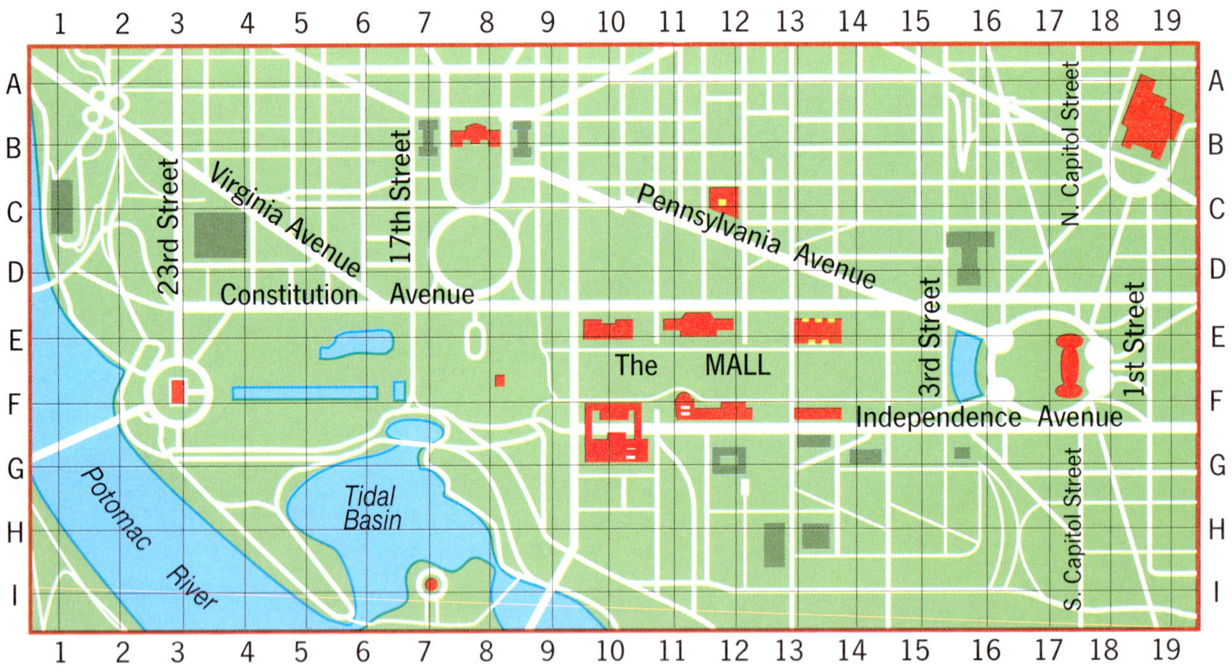

Map Index

Capitol	E 17
FBI Building	C 12
Jefferson Memorial	I 7
Lincoln Memorial	F 3
Museum of American History	E 10
Museum of Natural History	E 11
National Air and Space Museum	F 13
National Gallery of Art	E 13
Smithsonian Institution	F 11
Union Station	A 19
Washington Monument	F 8
White House	B 8

National Geography Standards: 1, 3
Basic Geography Skills: Analyzing geographic information and answering geographic questions
Geographic Theme: Location — Position on Earth's surface

Informal Assessment: Check to make sure students can use the index and grid to locate places on the map of Washington, D.C.

A. Use the map index and grid to find these places.

1. Lincoln Memorial F3
2. FBI Building C12
3. Smithsonian Institution F11

B. Use the map grid to identify these places.

1. What important home is found at B8? White House
2. A memorial to the third U.S. president is found at I7. What is its name?

   Jefferson Memorial
3. A major transportation center is located at A19. What is it?

   Union Station

C. Use the map index and grid to answer these questions about the Mall.

1. What is at the east end of the Mall? Capitol building
2. What is at the west end? Washington Monument
3. Identify four of the important buildings found along the Mall.

   (Answers might include: Smithsonian Institution, Museum of Natural History, National Gallery of Art, National Air and Space Museum, and Museum of American History.)

Activity Objective: Compare a planned and an unplanned community.
Cross-Curricular Connection: History – Understands the history of the local community; understands changes in land use and economic activities in the local community since its founding
Almanac: See page 126.

Lesson 5

ACTIVITY

Compare your community's history with the history of Washington, D.C.

Your Community: Was It Planned?

The BIG Geographic Question

How can you tell whether you live in a planned community?

From the article you learned how the community of Washington, D.C., was planned. The map skills lesson showed you how to use a grid system. Now find out about the history of your own community to figure out whether it was planned.

A. Answer these questions to find out about the history of your community.

(Answers to these questions should reflect information students find about the early history of their community.)

1. Who were the first people to settle in your community? ______________________

____

____

2. When was the community started? ______________________

____

____

3. Why was the community started? ______________________

____

____

National Geography Standards: 1, 3, 12
Basic Geography Skills: Acquiring and analyzing geographic information
Geographic Theme: Place – Physical and human characteristics

Informal Assessment: Have the class brainstorm to determine the answers to question B, and observe their answers.
Standardized Test-Format Assessment: See page 151.

B. Complete the chart below to compare facts about your community to Washington, D.C.

	History of Washington, D.C.	History of Your Community
Why was that location selected?	central location; close to water	(Students' answers should reflect information students find out about their community.)
What were its major physical features?	Potomac River	
What is the purpose of the community?	the capital of the new nation	
Were streets planned using a grid?	yes	
Were parks included in the plan?	yes	
Where are many important buildings located?	near or around the mall	

C. Think about how your community grew and complete the following.

(Students might work together on the maps of their community.)

1. Find or make a map of your community as it is today.
2. Tell how your community has grown. (Encourage students to share sources of information about the growth of their community and then compare conclusions.)

____

____

____

3. Do you think your community was planned?

____

____

____

____

Materials: index cards, information about your local community (such as physical features, important buildings, and so on)

Lesson Overview for pages 32–37: Students study written and graphic information about the geographical features that make four U.S. communities unique.
Cross-Curricular Connection: Science – Understands basic Earth processes, such as that wind, water, and ice constantly change Earth's surface

Lesson 6

Four Fabulous Communities

Wind has shaped the Arizona plateau.

As you read about these communities, think about the geographical features that make them unique.

Over 800 years ago the Hopi Native American tribe settled in the town of Oraibi, Arizona. This community is in the sandy red **plateaus**–or high, flat lands–of northern Arizona. There, wind and rivers have carved the land into amazing shapes, cutting steep canyons out of the red rock.

The Hopi make beautiful pottery. Its patterns and colors reflect the canyon walls and the colors of the rocks of the Arizona plateau.

Another state with a unique Native American community is Oklahoma. It has the largest Native American population in the United States. Each June the Red Earth Native American Cultural Festival is held in Oklahoma City. People from all over North America go to the festival.

More than fifty tornadoes roar through the state of Oklahoma each year.

Oklahoma is in the **plains.** This area of broad, flat land gets little rain, but there is lots of wind. No wonder the state song says "Oklahoma, where the wind comes sweepin' o'er the plain."

National Geography Standards: 4, 7
Basic Geographic Skills: Acquiring and analyzing geographic information
Geographic Theme: Place – Physical and human characteristics

Informal Assessment: Ask students to explain these terms: plateau (large area of high, flat land); plain (broad area of low, level land); lake (large body of water surrounded by land); hill (high landform not as tall as a mountain).

Water, not wind, makes Leech Lake in northern Minnesota special. For more than 400 years the Ojibway have gathered wild rice from the lake. They harvest the rice from canoes, knocking the grains into their boats as they glide through the quiet waters.

Northern Minnesota is full of rivers and lakes. Dense forests protect many kinds of wildlife. It's one of the few areas in the country where timber wolves still live.

Minnesota is known for its beautiful lakes.

Forests also cover the hills of western Virginia, where the town of Abingdon is located. The hills aren't high, but they're rugged. Long ago, it was hard to travel to get goods for the home. For this reason, families made most of their household items. Travel is easier now, but many residents still make traditional crafts.

These are just four examples of how physical features such as plateaus, plains, hills, rivers, and lakes can help make a place unique. In many communities in the United States, people use the physical features of their area to create items or events that they can share with people who do not live there.

The hills of western Virginia are rugged.

Program Resource: *National Geographic CD-ROM: Picture Atlas of the World; National Geographic Software: Zip Zap Map! USA.* Use to view the physical features of Arizona, Oklahoma, Minnesota, and Virginia.

Map Skills Objective: Differentiate between state capitals and major cities and their physical features.
Cross-Curricular Connection: Language Arts — Effectively gathers/uses information for research; asks and seeks to answer questions regarding the characteristics of people and places outside the local community
Almanac: See page 131.

Lesson 6

MAP SKILLS Using a Map to Locate Capital City Communities

Every state has many unique communities. But every state has only one capital city. A state's capital is the home of its government. It is where the state governor holds office and where the state legislature meets. These are some of the things that make a capital city unique. But, is the capital city representative of other unique communities in a state?

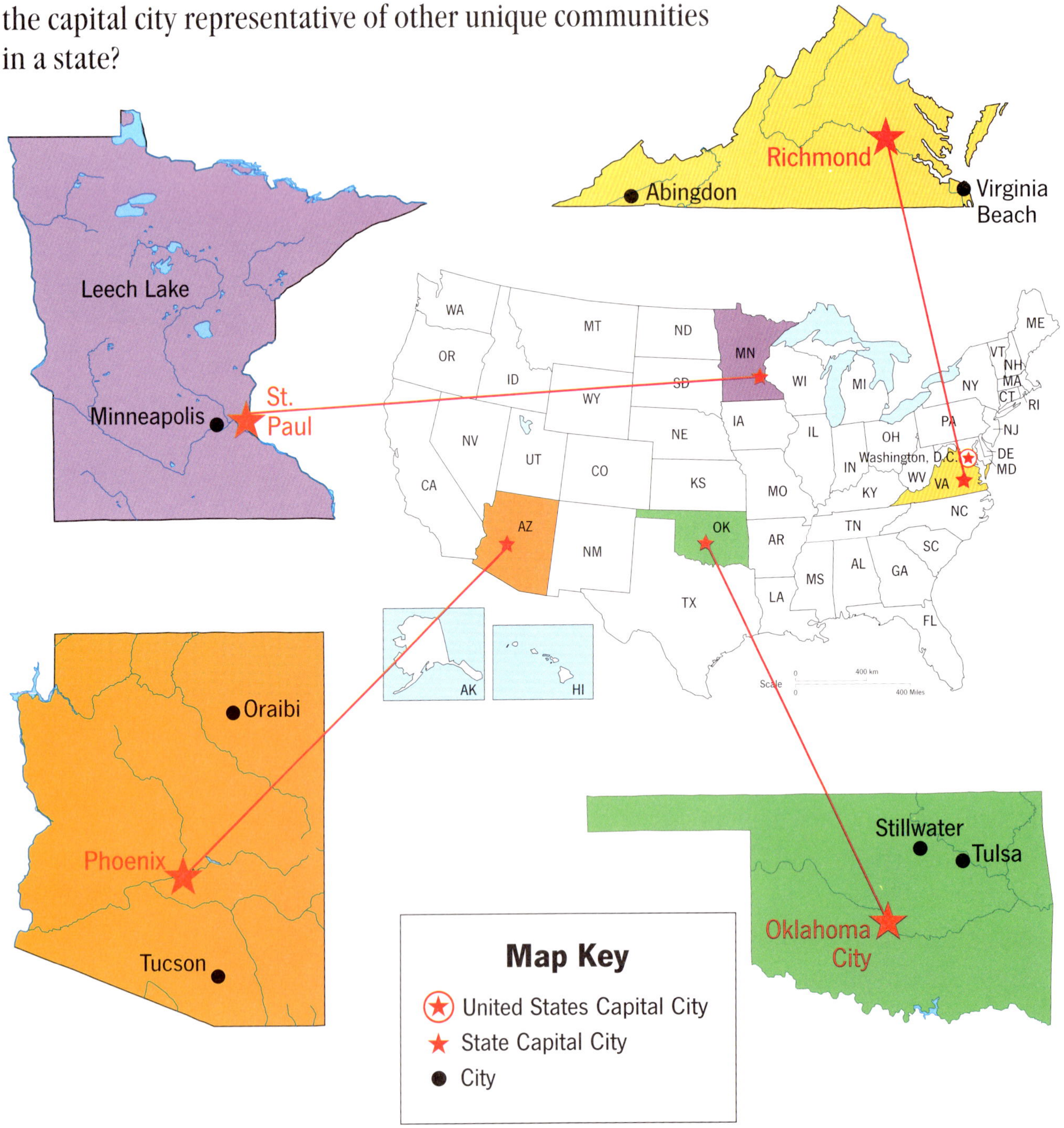

National Geography Standards: 1, 4, 8
Basic Geography Skills: Acquiring, analyzing, and organizing geographic information
Geographic Theme: Place — Physical and human characteristics

Informal Assessment: Have students demonstrate that they can use the map key to differentiate between the national capital and a state capital.

A. Different maps use different symbols to show the capital city of a state or country. You can find each symbol in the map key. Look at the map of the United States. Find the map key.

1. What is the symbol for the United States capital? ⊛ ______

2. What is the symbol for the state capitals? ★ ______

B. Find the states of Arizona, Minnesota, Oklahoma, and Virginia on the map. Use the information on the map to find each state's capital and the community described in the article for each state. Record your information on the chart below.

State	Capital City	Community Featured in Article
Arizona	Phoenix	Oraibi
Minnesota	St. Paul	Leech Lake
Oklahoma	Oklahoma City	Oklahoma City
Virginia	Richmond	Abingdon

C. Choose one of the capital cities you listed above to learn more about. Look in the Almanac for information on the state's capital. Complete the T-chart below by listing information about the capital city and the featured city. Note any similarities and differences. Based on the information you have collected, decide whether the state's capital city is representative of other unique communities in the state. (An example follows.)

Capital City	Featured City
Phoenix, Arizona • located in the Salt River Valley • a flat region with low mountains • warm, dry climate • large vacation industry • Hohokam Native Americans lived there	Oraibi, Arizona • located in northern Arizona • plateaus, or high, flat land • strong winds shape the land • steep canyons of red rock • Hopi Native Americans lived there

Activity Objective: Recognize the geographical features of one's own community that make it a special and attractive place to live and visit.
Cross-Curricular Connection: Language Arts — Effectively gathers/uses information by asking and seeking answers to questions about people/places in the local community
Almanac: See page 131.

Lesson 6

Activity

Advertise physical features of your community that attract people to live or visit there.

Your Community: What Are Its Features?

The BIG Geographic Question

What physical features of a community make it a unique place?

In the article you read about some of the physical features that make four communities special. In the map skills lesson you located state capitals and looked at whether they were representative of other communities in the state. Now plan and present an advertisement that highlights a physical feature of your community to attract people to come there.

A. Think about the features of the communities you read about on pages 32–33.

1. Use the chart below to list the important physical features of each community. An example has been done for you.

State	Arizona	Minnesota	Oklahoma	Virginia
Community	Oraibi	Leech Lake	Oklahoma City	Abingdon
Features	• sandy red plateaus • wind and rivers carve canyons through red rock	lakes, rivers, forests	plains	mountains, forests

National Geography Standards: 4, 16
Basic Geography Skills: Organizing geographic information and answering geographic questions
Geographic Theme: Place — Physical and human characteristics

Informal Assessment: Help students assess their advertisements based on special features highlighted, design appeal, and whether they might attract people to their community.
Standardized Test-Format Assessment: See page 152.

2. How do these features help make the communities special places to live or visit?

Oraibi: majestic landscape, Hopi Native American community, beautiful pottery; Leech Lake: wild rice, Ojibway community lifestyles, beautiful forests; Oklahoma City: Native American community and celebrations; Abingdon: mountain towns, forests, traditional crafts

B. Think about your community and complete the following.

1. Make a chart showing the special physical features of your own state, its capital city, or your community. Some of these physical features might include rivers, lakes, forests, mountains, or plains. Some other features might include the different groups of people who live there or fun things to do there. Jot down your notes below. (Students' answers should accurately reflect their communities.)

Your Community's Name	
Special Physical Features	
Other Special Features	

2. How do these features make your community special?

(Students' answers should accurately reflect their communities.)

C. Now plan and present an advertisement for your community. Your advertisement can be a poster, a flyer, a TV commercial, or a radio commercial. It might include a picture and a written description of the physical feature that makes your community a unique place to live or visit.

(Make sure students' ads include a description of the physical feature(s) that make their community special. You may wish to invite students to share their commercials with the class.)

Materials: information about your local community

Lesson Overview for pages 38–43: Students use written and graphic material about Jamestown as an example of why early communities were settled where they were.
Cross-Curricular Connection: History – Understands how communities in North America varied long ago

Lesson 7

Adventure to the New World

As you read about Jamestown, think about the role geography played in its settlement.

Jamestown has been restored to the way archaeologists believe the original village looked.

Would you dare to leave everything behind and travel to an unknown place far away? How would you know where to settle? What would you look for to help you survive? In December of 1606 three small wooden ships left London, England, heading for the New World. The people on board traveled through good and bad weather. They were hoping for a better life in the New World. Many believed they would find silver or gold and get rich quickly.

The journey was long and hard. After more than four months, the colonists finally spotted land. Did they anchor their ships near the first place they saw? No. They followed the James River until they came upon a little peninsula. A **peninsula** is an area of land surrounded by water on three sides. The colonists thought this would be a safe location, since it would be hard for attackers to see from the ocean. It would also be possible to defend from both land and sea. In addition, there were many trees to use for building the things necessary to survive.

National Geography Standards: 4, 12, 17
Basic Geography Skill: Acquiring geographic information
Geographic Theme: Movement – Humans interacting on Earth

Informal Assessment: Have students share how they think the colonists would have described the place where they settled Jamestown in 1607.

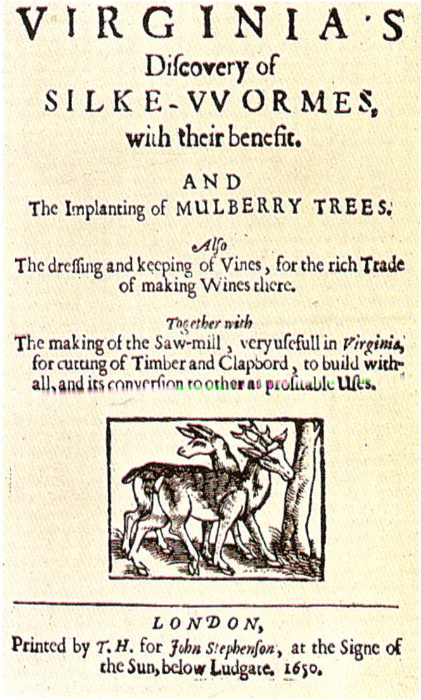
VIRGINIA'S
Discovery of
SILKE-VVORMES,
with their benefit.
AND
The Implanting of MULBERRY TREES.
Also
The dressing and keeping of Vines, for the rich Trade of making Wines there.
Together with
The making of the Saw-mill, very usefull in *Virginia*, for cutting of Timber and Clapbord, to build withall, and its conversion to other as profitable Uses.

LONDON,
Printed by *T. H.* for *John Stephenson*, at the Signe of the Sun, below Ludgate. 1650.

The colonists settled on the peninsula and named it Jamestown. This settlement was named after the English king, James I.

Was this location a good choice? Sadly, it was not. The ground was swampy. The only drinking water was from the river, which was full of germs. Many people became sick and died. Diseases, starvation, and attacks by Native Americans also took the lives of many colonists.

In spite of the problems, Jamestown did survive and was the first permanent English settlement in North America. It became an important Virginia farming community, as well as a model for early government in America.

The peninsula that was the site of the original Jamestown settlement is now an **island.** An island is an area of land surrounded by water on all sides. Much of the original land has been washed away by currents in the James River. Luckily, however, the Jamestown settlement has been restored to the way it looked in the 1600s. Each year thousands of people visit Jamestown, Virginia, to see, taste, touch, and hear what life was like when our country was just beginning.

The harbor of Jamestown, Virginia, as seen from an airplane.

Learn More About It: *National Geographic Historical Atlas of the United States,* pp. 80–81

Lesson 7 MAP SKILLS
Using a Historical Map to Get Information About the Past

A **historical map** gives information about the past. It can give information about the physical and human features that caused things to happen in the past.

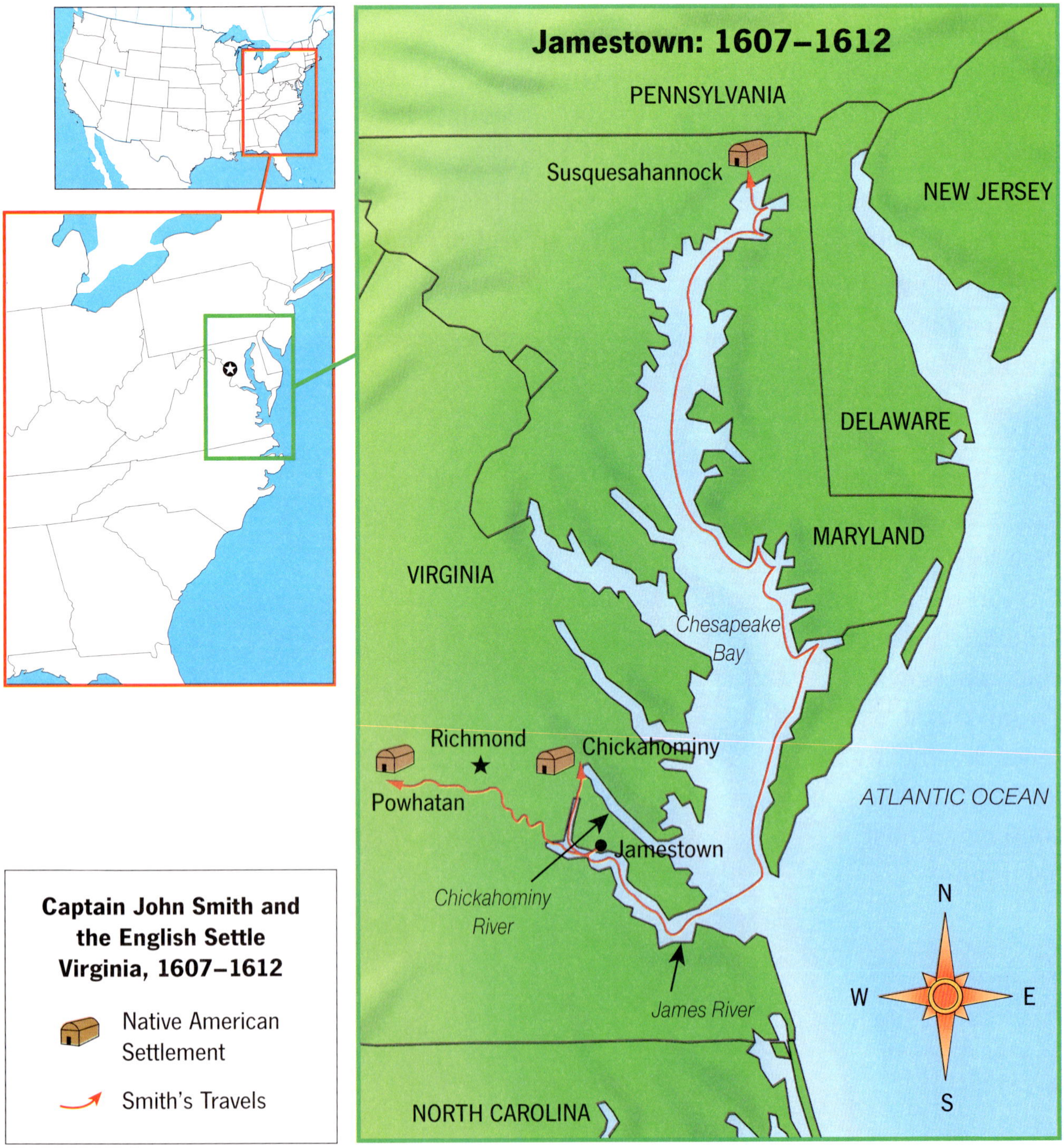

National Geography Standards: 1, 4, 12, 17
Basic Geography Skills: Asking geographic questions, analyzing geographic information, and answering geographic questions
Geographic Theme: Place – Physical and human characteristics

Informal Assessment: To emphasize the significance of waterways in the settlement of communities, have students use a historical state or United States map to find as many cities as they can that are located on water.

A. Look at the map of early Virginia.

1. Circle Jamestown.
2. Write down the time in history that this map is showing. 1607–1612
3. Circle the Chesapeake Bay and Atlantic Ocean.
4. Mark an *X* on the early Native American settlements.
   (Students should mark Susquesahannock, Powhatan, and Chickahominy.)

B. Look at the map and complete the following.

1. Circle the names of the bodies of water you see on the map.
2. Write the names of the bodies of water.

   a. Atlantic Ocean

   b. Chesapeake Bay

   c. James River

   d. Chickahominy River

3. Trace the peninsula on which Jamestown is located. (Make sure students correctly trace the peninsula.)
4. Write the names of the bodies of water Captain Smith followed to get from Jamestown to:

   a. Susquesahannock (səhs-kwəh-səh-HAN-ək)

   James River, Chesapeake Bay, James River

   b. Powhatan (pow-HAT-əhn)

   James River

   c. Chickahominy (chi-kə-HÄ-mə-nē)

   James River, Chickahominy River

5. Was the peninsula a good location to settle Jamestown? Why or why not?

   (If students said yes, the reason might be: Water provided a way to travel and move goods from place to place. If students said no, the reason might be: The water was not safe to drink.)

6. Why was it important to be located near water in the early days of the Jamestown settlement?

   Waterways were used for transportation, exploration, and trade.

Activity Objective: Consider the reasons for staying in or leaving an early settlement, and make a decision.
Cross-Curricular Connection: History — Understands how communities in North America varied long ago
Almanac: See pages 122–123.

Lesson 7

ACTIVITY

Decide whether you would have left or stayed in Jamestown.

What Would YOU Do?

The BIG Geographic Question

Would you have remained in Jamestown or gone back to England in 1607?

A. **List on the idea web below characteristics of life in early Jamestown. Include both positive and negative characteristics. Add more spaces if you need to.** (Characteristics of Jamestown might include the following.)

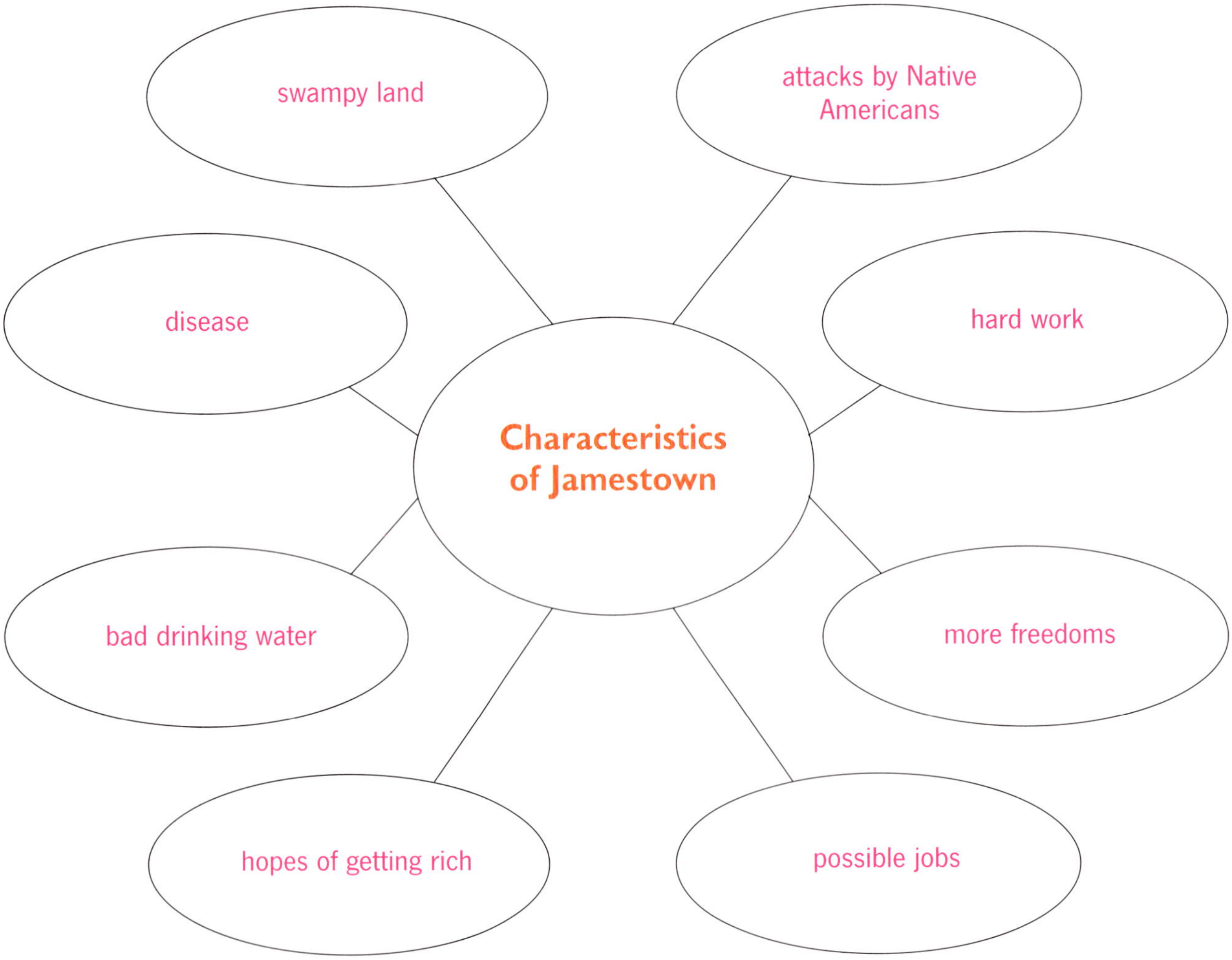

National Geography Standards: 4, 12, 17
Basic Geography Skills: Acquiring, analyzing, and organizing geographic information
Geographic Theme: Movement — Humans interacting on Earth

Informal Assessment: Have students compare their reasons and decisions for staying or leaving. Discuss them as a class.
Standardized Test-Format Assessment: See page 153.

B. Use the chart below to take notes on what the living conditions were like in Jamestown in 1607.

	Good	Bad
Land Features	many trees	swampy land
Water Features	many rivers for travel and transport	bad drinking water
Other Features	more freedoms, hopes of getting rich, adventure, possible jobs	disease, attack by Native Americans

C. Using the information you collected, list reasons you would leave or stay in Jamestown.

(Students' reasons might include the following.)

Reasons to Leave	Reasons to Stay
not enough food	promise of riches
bad drinking water	adventure in a new land
wet and swampy ground	many more freedoms
hard work	possible jobs
harsh weather	trees for building

D. Pretend to be an early Jamestown settler. With your classmates, stage a town meeting to discuss whether to leave or stay in the community. Listen carefully to the ideas of others. When the meeting is over, think about the arguments you heard both for staying and for leaving. What did you decide? Write your decision and the reasons for it on the lines below.

(Make sure students' decisions and reasons are appropriate to the time in history.)

Lesson Overview for pages 44–49: Students study written and graphic material to understand how the geography of the past played a key role in the lives of early Native American communities.
Cross-Curricular Connection: History — Understands how communities in North America varied long ago; knows the geographic settings, economic activities, food, clothing, homes, crafts, and rituals of prehistoric Native American societies

Lesson 8

Our First Communities

As you read about the first North Americans, think about how they used the land to live.

Thousands of years before the first Europeans arrived in North America, the first Americans traveled across the land and settled. These Native Americans of long ago **adapted** to, or learned to live in, the natural environments. Some groups hunted animals and gathered food. Others grew crops. From the land and its resources, they made many of the everyday objects they needed.

The Iroquois of long ago made colorful wampum belts from shells and beads. They wove baskets and made masks from cornhusks. From the trunks of large trees, they carved masks and wooden bowls. The Iroquois used bark from the oak, birch, and elm trees of the northeast woodlands to make canoes. The homes of the Iroquois were made of wooden poles covered with bark and were filled with objects they made from the land.

Square Tower House, Mesa Verde Ruins. No one knows why the Anasazi, an ancient people, moved from the cliff dwellings 700 years ago.

National Geography Standards: 4, 5, 12, 17, 18
Basic Geography Skills: Acquiring and analyzing geographic information
Geographic Themes: Human/Environmental Interaction — Relationship within places; Place — Physical and human characteristics

Informal Assessment: Have students categorize objects Native Americans made from plants, animals, and earth by completing a chart as follows.

Plant	Animal	Earth
baskets, masks, canoes, houses, medicine	clothing, tepees, tools, dolls	adobe houses, clay pots

The Sioux Native American tribe of long ago made their home in the Great Plains. Many of the objects they made came from the animals that lived on the plains. These Native Americans carved cups, bowls, and tools from animal bones. The Sioux made leggings, shirts, and moccasins from deerskin. They used buffalo hides draped over wooden poles to form tepees. These Native Americans of long ago found a use for almost every part of the buffalo to make everyday objects like drums, pots, and balls for play. They even used buffalo hooves to make rattles and sewed with buffalo sinew for thread and bones for needles.

Cliff dwellings were the homes of the Anasazi people of long ago. The Anasazi made their homes almost entirely from the earth. They used the desert sandstone to make bricks for their homes. These bricks were held together with **adobe,** a sandy clay mixed with straw. The Anasazi discovered that adobe was easy to mold and would not shrink in the hot, dry weather. These Native Americans of the southwest also made beautiful pots from clay. They often painted elaborate geometric designs on them.

Today we can learn much about the very first North Americans by studying the **artifacts,** or tools, shelters, crafts, clothing, and other objects, they made. Artifacts from the past provide us with the clues we need to put together a picture of life in North America long ago. They are clues to how Native Americans, like other early Americans, adapted to their environment.

Learn More About It: *National Geographic Historical Atlas of the United States,* pp. 32–35

Map Skills Objective: Use a map to identify regional groups of Native Americans and the physical characteristics of the various regions in which they lived.
Cross-Curricular Connection: History — Understands how communities in North America varied long ago; knows the geographic settings, economic activities, food, clothing, homes, crafts, and rituals of prehistoric Native American societies

Lesson 8

MAP SKILLS Using a Map to Show Land and People

Some map keys use color to show the landforms and water forms or to show where groups of people live. Other map keys use symbols to show the same information.

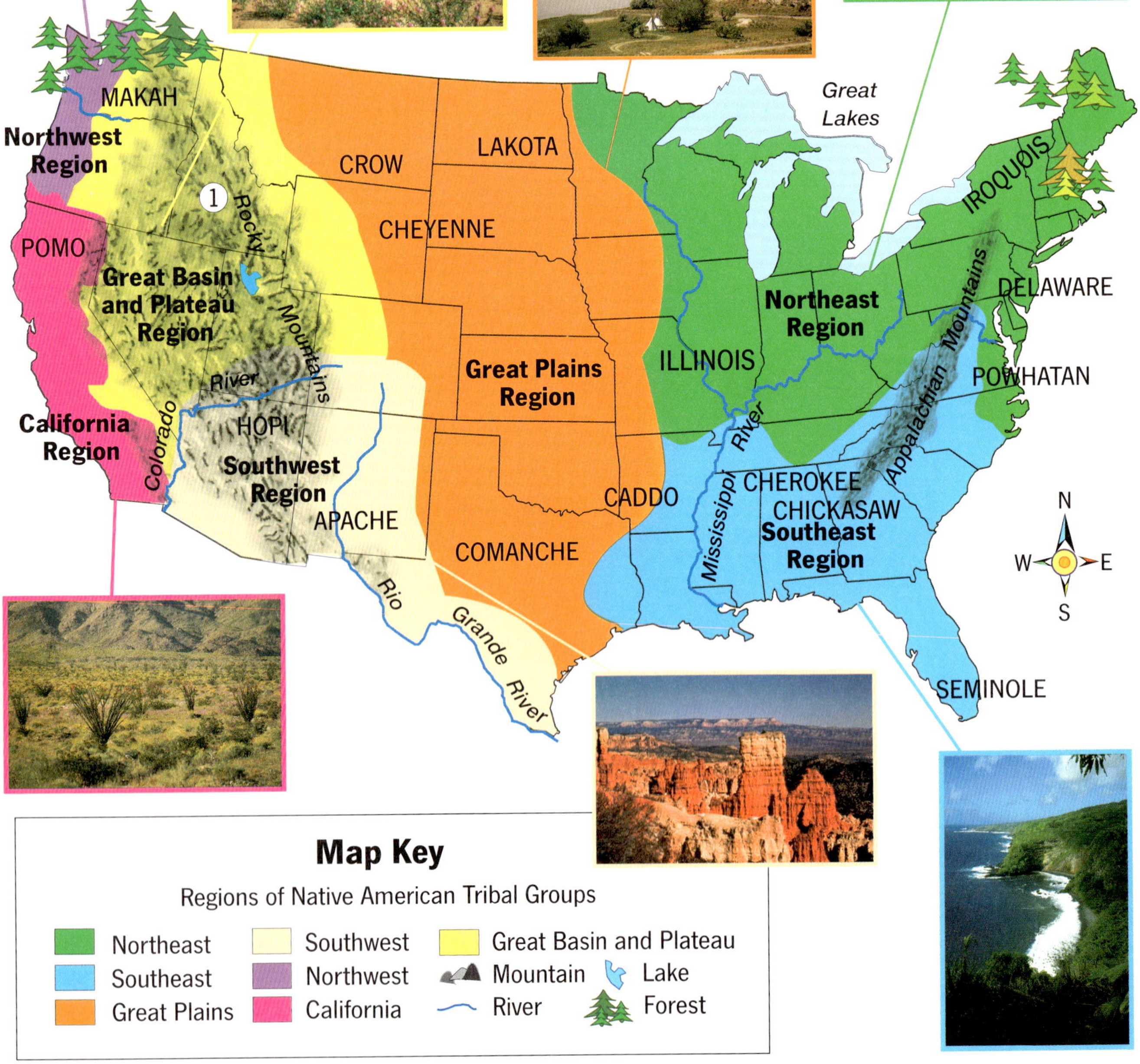

National Geography Standards: 1, 4, 5
Basic Geography Skills: Asking geographic questions, analyzing geographic information, and answering geographic questions
Geographic Theme: Place — Physical and human characteristics; Regions — How they form and change

Informal Assessment: Check to make sure students understand how to use the map keys for symbols and colors to find the location of landforms and tribes.

A. Look at the map key. Put the appropriate number on the map to show where each of the following physical features is located. An example has been done for you. (Make sure students put numbers in the right places.)

1. mountain
2. river
3. lake
4. forest
5. Great Plains
6. ocean

B. Look at the map and map key to regional groups.

1. Which color shows where the Iroquois tribe lived? red

2. The southwestern United States has many desert areas. Which Native Americans of long ago lived in this area? (Possible answers include the Hopi and the Apache.)

3. Which groups of Native Americans might have used resources from the ocean? (Possible answers include the Chinook, the Maka, and the Delaware.)

4. On what river might Native Americans from the Great Plains region have traveled north and south? They might have traveled on the Mississippi River.

5. Which groups obtained their resources from forests?
(Possible answers include the Iroquois and the Chinook.)

6. What three regions were divided by mountains?
The Great Plains, the Southwest, and Great Basin and Plateau.

7. How do you know that the Chickasaw and the Cherokee came from the southeast?
They are shown to have lived in the green area on the map. Green stands for southeast.

8. If you traveled by land from your state to visit a Native American tribe of long ago in the northwest, what landforms or water forms would you have had to cross? If you lived in the northwest, think about traveling to visit a tribe in the southeast. Explain whether your trip would be difficult.
(Students' answers should reflect an understanding of how to read a map for the location of various landforms such as mountains, rivers, and plains.)

Activity Objective: Use geographical characteristics of a regional area and the tools and artifacts of different Native American tribes as clues about the areas in which they lived and their lifestyles.
Cross-Curricular Connection: History – Understands how to analyze chronological relationships and patterns; knows how to interpret time lines
Almanac: See pages 118–121.

Lesson 8

Activity

Find out about the ways of living of Native American tribes long ago.

Digging for Clues

The BIG Geographic Question

What can you find out about the first Native Americans by studying the artifacts they left behind?

From the article you learned about the tools, crafts, clothing, and shelters of some Native American tribes of long ago. The map skills lesson showed you where they lived and some of the landforms found in those regions. Use these clues and information you find in the Almanac to learn about the way of living of a Native American tribe of long ago.

A. Complete the following.

1. List the names of Native American tribes you have read about.

Apache	Kickapoo
Cherokee	Miami
Chinook	Navajo
Hopi	Pueblo
Iroquois	Sioux

2. Write down the name of a Native American tribe that you would like to learn more about.

(Make sure students choose a tribe.)

National Geography Standards: 4, 11, 12, 17
Basic Geography Skills: Acquiring and analyzing geographic information and answering geographic questions
Geographic Themes: Human/Environmental Interaction – Relationship within places; Place – Physical and human characteristics

Informal Assessment: Have students compare and contrast their posters.
Standardized Test-Format Assessment: See page 154.

B. Answer the following questions about the tribe you have chosen.

1. In what region of the United States did the tribe you selected live?

   (Make sure students indicate the correct region for the tribe they selected.)

2. What were some of the landforms or water forms found where this tribe lived?

   (Landforms should include those shown on the map, such as mountains, forests, plains, and deserts, and water forms such as rivers and lakes.)

3. What was the climate of their land like? (Make sure students indicate the correct climate for their chosen region.)

4. What kinds of resources were found there? (Resources could include water, land, animals, trees, soil, and rocks.)

5. How did the tribe obtain and use these resources? (Possible answers include hunting, carving, digging, chopping, or gathering.)

C. Make some additional notes about the tribe that you have chosen using the article and Almanac. Make a chart like the one below and record your information on it. (Sample information is provided.)

Native American Tribe Name and Region Iroquois of the northeast region

Shelter	Clothing	Food	Tools	Crafts	Movement
• wooden poles covered with bark	• wampum belts • animal skins	• beaver • deer • bear • rabbit • muskrat • corn	• stone axes • wooden tools	• masks • wooden bowls • baskets • cornhusk dolls	• canoes made of birch bark • walking with moccasins or snowshoes

D. Use the clues that you gathered to tell a story about the life of the Native American tribe that you studied. Design a poster that shows what you discovered. Include details about how the people worked and lived. Plan your poster first, then make it. Include it as part of a classroom display about early life in America.

(Students' displays might include illustrations, diagrams, and captions. Dioramas could be constructed from materials such as shoe boxes, wood, bark, leather, paper, string, and clay.)

Lesson Overview for pages 50–55: Students study written and graphic information about St. Augustine as an example of how the resources of a place were used and influenced settlement there.
Cross-Curricular Connection: History — Understands how communities in North America varied long ago

Lesson 9

A Town Is Born

The Story of St. Augustine

As you read about St. Augustine, think about how its physical and cultural features and resources are important to the community there.

During the 1500s only Native Americans lived in what is now the United States. Later, sailors from Europe stumbled upon this unknown land. After that, many European countries sent people to explore and settle this "New World." They hoped to find gold, spices, and other riches.

Explorers came from Spain and France to what is now Florida. When the French built a fort in northern Florida, the Spanish were upset. The fort was on land Spain believed it owned. Spain was afraid that the French would attack Spanish ships.

Spain's king, Philip II, sent Pedro Menéndez de Avilés to destroy the French fort and start a town. Besides sailors and soldiers, Menéndez brought settlers.

After Menéndez destroyed the fort, he found a good harbor dotted with small islands. These islands were excellent places to watch for enemy ships. They also had stone and timber that could be used for building.

This early picture shows the Castillo de San Marcos.

National Geography Standards: 4, 12, 16
Basic Geography Skills: Acquiring and analyzing geographic information
Geographic Theme: Human/Environmental Interaction — Relationship within places; Place — Physical and human characteristics

In 1565 Menéndez started the town of St. Augustine at this wonderful harbor. The soldiers built a wooden fort where they kept watch. The settlers built homes. The town was the first permanent European settlement in the New World.

The Castillo de San Marcos was shaped like a huge rectangle with a sea-filled moat and a drawbridge to keep out enemies.

The wooden fort kept burning down, so the people of early St. Augustine decided to use **coquina** stone from a nearby island to build a new fort, the Castillo de San Marcos. St. Augustine slowly grew. Today it is a small city and the oldest settlement in North America.

St. Augustine is proud of its interesting past.

Lesson 9

MAP SKILLS

Using a Map Key to Identify Resources of an Area

Maps can show the **resources** found in an area. Resources are things that people use, such as plants, animals, and minerals. A symbol can be used on a map to show where each resource is found. The map key usually shows what each symbol stands for.

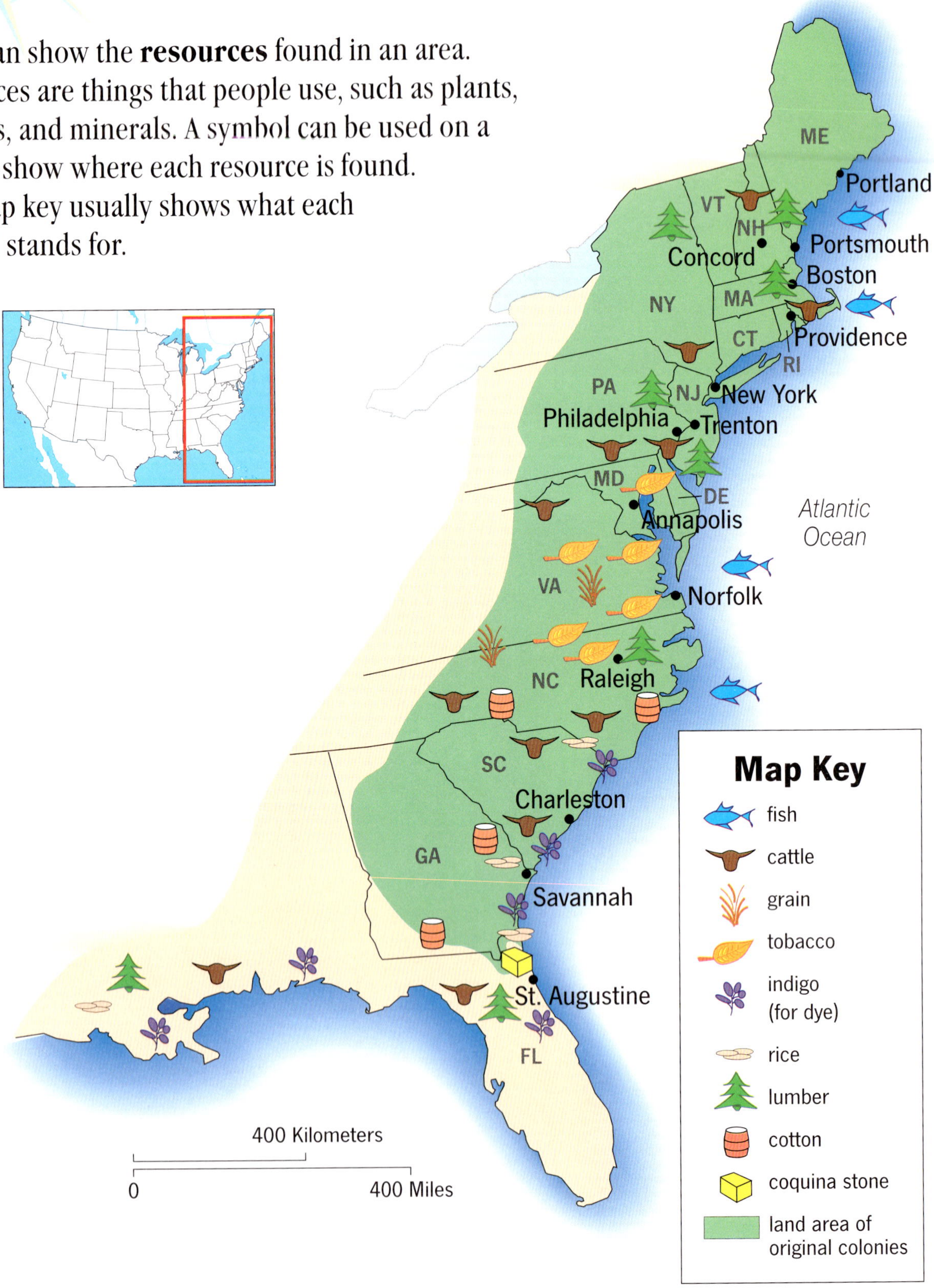

National Geography Standards: 1, 16, 17
Basic Geography Skills: Asking and answering geographic questions
Geographic Theme: Place — Physical and human characteristics

Informal Assessment: Check to make sure students can identify the resource symbols used on the map and explain the use of each resource.

A. Look at the map on page 72 of the United States in the 1700s. Circle the following: (Make sure students have circled the correct items on the map.)

1. map key
2. St. Augustine
3. Boston
4. rice symbols
5. cattle symbols
6. Atlantic Ocean

B. Look at the symbols on the map key and answer the following.

1. Write down what each symbol represents.

   a.  is the symbol for lumber.

   b.  is the symbol for fish.

   c.  is the symbol for tobacco.

2. Find Charleston on the map. In what early colony is Charleston located?

   South Carolina

3. Look at the symbols on the map near Charleston. What resources can be found in or near Charleston?

   cattle   indigo

4. What towns have indigo as an important resource?

   Savannah   Charleston   St. Augustine

5. What town has coquina stone as an important resource?

   St. Augustine

6. Which resource is found the most often on the map?

   cattle

7. What could the people of North Carolina have done with their resources?

   (Students' answers might include: build homes and ships with the lumber; make cloth from the cotton; and eat and export the rice and grain.)

Activity Objective: Compare resources of communities of the past to those of today.
Cross-Curricular Connection: History – Understands changes in land use and economic activities in the local community since its founding
Almanac: See page 124.

Lesson 9

ACTIVITY

Find out what resources are found in your community.

Your Community's Resources

The BIG Geographic Question

How have local resources been used by your community?

From the article you learned how the town of St. Augustine was started and that its resources were used to build forts and homes. The map skills lesson showed you where different resources were found in different places in the United States long ago. Find out what resources are located in your community. Remember, people are resources, too.

A. Answer the following questions about your community.

1. What farm crops are grown in your community? ______________________

(Make sure the crops students list are grown in their community.)

2. What farm animals are raised in your community? ______________________

(Make sure the animals students listed are raised in their community.)

3. How do some of the people in your community earn a living? ______________________

(Make sure students list occupations that exist in their community.)

4. Write *yes* in the blank if the following are found in or near your community.

   lake, river, ocean ______________

   woods ______________

   quarries or mines ______________

   stores, hospitals, schools ______________

National Geography Standards: 4, 14, 16
Basic Geography Skills: Asking and answering geographic questions and organizing and analyzing geographic information
Geographic Theme: Place – Physical and human characteristics

Informal Assessment: Have students compare and contrast their community maps to their questions and answers about their community.
Standardized Test-Format Assessment: See page 155.

B. Write four resources found in your community. Then write how each resource is used. (Students should list four resources found in their community and possible uses of each.)

Resource: ______________________ Use: ______________________

Resource: ______________________ Use: ______________________

Resource: ______________________ Use: ______________________

Resource: ______________________ Use: ______________________

C. Using the chart below, compare your community's resources with those of St. Augustine. First write the four resources you listed above. Then put a check mark in each box if your community or St. Augustine has that resource. (Make sure students have accurately completed the chart.)

Resource	Your Community	St. Augustine
	✓	
	✓	
	✓	
	✓	
stone		✓
lumber		✓
water (nearby ocean, lake, or river)		✓

D. Talk to friends and family members or go to the library to find out whether your answers were correct. Use or draw a map of your community showing where its important resources are located. Write a short description of why these resources are important to your community.

(Students' maps should reflect knowledge of their community. Answers should reveal an understanding of the importance of local resources to a community.)

Materials: information about your local community (including resources such as crops, animals, natural resources, and people)

Lesson Overview for pages 56–61: Students study written and graphic materials to learn how and why rural communities are geographically important.
Cross-Curricular Connection: History – Understands the history of the local community; understands the differences between products and services now and long ago

Lesson 10

FOODS AND FESTIVALS

As you read about rural communities, think about how the people who live there interact with the physical geography around them.

Who grows the food you eat? Farmers across the country do. What farmers raise depends on what grows well on the land and in the climate where they live. Half the land in the United States is used as farmland. Because there are so many kinds of soil and climate regions throughout the country, farmers can grow many of the things you like to eat. They can also grow many products that can be used to make other things you need, such as cotton to make fabric for clothing.

If the soil in an area is sandy, farmers there can grow peanuts. If the climate in an area is rainy, farmers there can raise rice, corn, and cotton. If the growing season in an area is long and warm, farmers in that area can grow oranges.

On small farms, such as ones in New England, farmers might raise poultry. On large ranches in the plains and mountain states, farmers often raise wheat and cattle. Do you like salmon or lobster? Fishers who live near oceans, lakes, and rivers catch most of the seafood that you eat.

National Geography Standards: 4, 12, 16
Basic Geography Skills: Asking and answering geographic questions
Geographic Theme: Human/Environmental Interaction – Relationship within places

Informal Assessment: Have students see how many things they can list that affect the kinds of products that come from the land or water in an area. They should list type of soil, climate, amount of land available, and amount of water available.

Rural communities are very important ones. The families in these communities take pride in the fruits, flowers, grains, and vegetables they grow and the animals they raise. Often these communities have fairs and festivals to show and celebrate the products that are important to them as well as us. The products that rural communities raise and the fairs and festivals they have are an important way that people interact with the geography around them.

CORN PALACE FESTIVAL
Mitchell, SD
Sept. 8–17

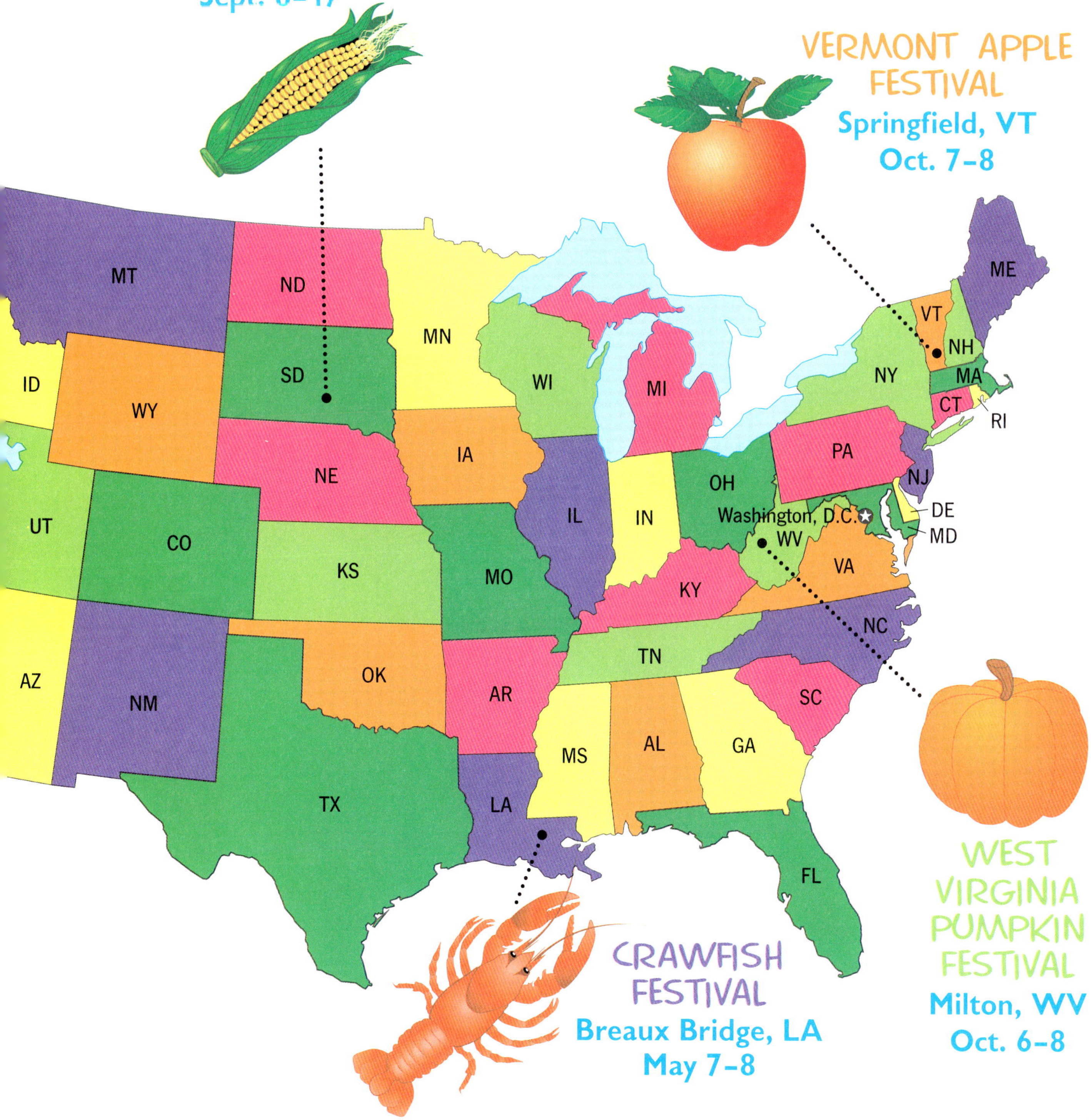

Map Skills Objective: Use a map to understand and identify various geographically significant aspects of different rural communities.
Cross-Curricular Connection: Language Arts – Effectively gathers/uses information for research; asks and seeks to answer questions regarding the characteristics of people and places outside the local community

Lesson 10

MAP SKILLS

Using a Map Key to Find Out Where Products Come From

A map key explains the symbols used on a map. Sometimes symbols look like the things they stand for. A map key can help us understand a map.

Regions and Resources

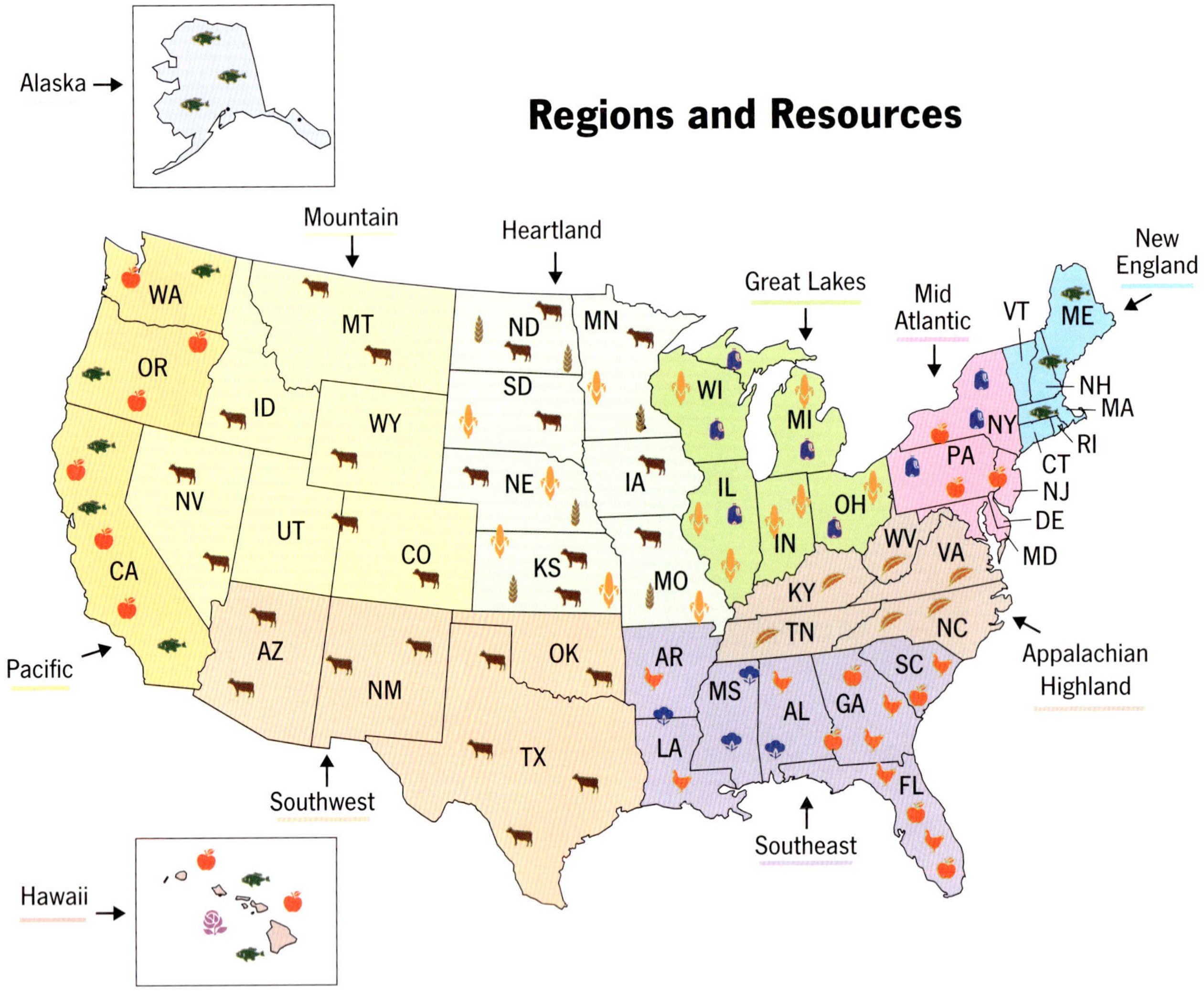

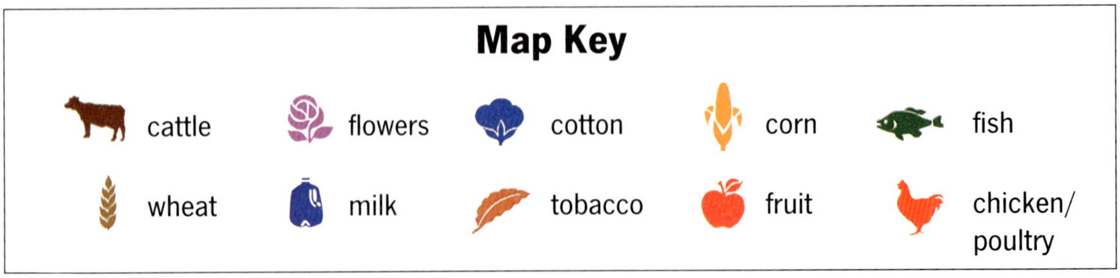

National Geography Standards: 1, 4, 5, 16
Basic Geography Skills: Acquiring and analyzing geographic information
Geographic Themes: Human/Environmental Interaction – Relationship within places; Location – Position on Earth's surface

Informal Assessment: Check to make sure students can use the symbols on the map to identify the locations of particular resources. They should visually estimate the data on the map in order to answer question C.

A. Cover up the map key on page 58. Now look at the symbols below. Write what each symbol stands for.

 cattle

 wheat

 corn

 fruit

 fish

 flowers

 milk

 chicken, poultry

 tobacco

 cotton

B. Write the name of a product that comes from each region listed below. Then write the states where each product is found.

Region	Product	State
New England	fish	ME, VT, MA, NH
Mid-Atlantic	milk, fruit	NY, PA, NJ
Southeast	poultry, cotton, fruit	AR, LA, MS, AL, GA, SC, FL
Heartland	cattle, corn, wheat	ND, SD, NE, KS, MN, IA, MO
Southwest	cattle	TX, NM, AZ
Pacific	fish, fruit	WA, CA, OR
Alaska	fish	AK
Hawaii	fish, fruit, flowers	HI

C. List the regions that produce the most:

cattle Heartland, Mountain, Southwest

corn Great Lakes, Heartland

tobacco Appalachian Highland

Activity Objective: Plan an event to exhibit the things that rural communities are known for and proud of.
Cross-Curricular Connection: Language Arts — Effectively gathers/uses information for research purposes about people and places within (or outside of) the local community
Almanac: See pages 111 and 126.

Lesson 10

Activity

Plan a fair to show the products a rural community might be known for and proud of.

Come to the Fair

The BIG Geographic Question

How is a fair or festival in a rural community an example of people interacting with the environment?

From the article you learned of some rural communities that hold fairs and festivals. The map skills lesson showed you products people grow on farmlands or catch in nearby waters. Now plan a fair to display a product of which a rural community is proud.

A. Use information from the article, the map, and the Almanac to help you choose a place and a product.

1. Choose a small town. (Students might choose a location that was highlighted in the article on pages 56–57 or one they have visited or heard about.)

2. Describe the location of the town. (Students should give the geographic location of the town they selected.)

3. Write the name of a product that is important to the town.
(Students should use the map or photographs to name a product important to the community.)

4. Tell whether the product grows on the land or comes from the water.
(Students' answers might include: crops, animals, flowers, and trees grow on land; fish live in water.)

B. Explain why you chose the place and product.

(Possible answers might include liking the product or knowing someone who lives in the region it comes from.)

National Geography Standards: 6, 16
Basic Geography Skills: Asking and answering geographic questions and acquiring and analyzing geographic information
Geographic Theme: Human/Environmental Interaction — Relationship within places

Informal Assessment: After students complete section C, observe whether they need additional explanation of the suggested events. Take a field trip to a local festival or ask students who have attended one to share their experiences.
Standardized Test-Format Assessment: See page 156.

C. Read the events on the checklist below. Decide which ones you will have at your fair and write *yes* or *no* in that column on the chart. Describe the events you will have at the fair. Remember to feature the local product. (The description of each event should reflect the featured product.)

Event	Yes or No	Description
parade		
displays		
floats		
food		
games		
posters		
music		
contests		
craft booths		
sales		
speakers		
the mayor		

D. Make a poster to advertise your festival. Include these details.

- festival name
- place
- date
- events
- artwork

(The festival name, place, events, and product should be on the poster. Note whether the poster shows an awareness of the growing season or harvest time.)

Materials: drawing paper, markers, crayons

Lesson 11

A City Comes to Life

As you read about the urban community of St. Louis, think about what makes up a city.

St. Louis, Missouri, is in the heart of the United States. It was once mostly **prairie**—fertile land where grass grew eight feet tall. How and why did St. Louis change from prairie land, to a small town, to a major city?

Like many major cities, St. Louis grew into a bustling city partly because of its location near major waterways. Settlers, traders, explorers, trappers, and gold seekers of long ago found the area easy to reach. St. Louis began as a trading center and grew into a city.

Major cities that are located on important waterways often become big manufacturing centers. Many people move from rural areas to the cities because they can find jobs there. Then shops, stores, restaurants, schools, and hospitals spring up. As more people come to find work, the city keeps growing.

Being located near water and having a reliable system of transportation play key roles in which places become cities. People and culture, jobs and recreational activities, and business and trade are also very important things that make a city grow.

Scientists and engineers work in high-technology industries.

Informal Assessment: Have students jot down all the things they find in a city that they did not see in the rural areas they read about. Possible answers include skyscrapers, factories, large stores, interstate highways, professional sports, and a symphony orchestra.

Two mighty rivers, the Mississippi and the Missouri, meet just north of St. Louis. Eight bridges span the Mississippi River which is the site of the St. Louis Gateway Arch.

Program Resource: *National Geographic Picture Atlas of Our Fifty States*, pp. 52–55, 230–233; *National Geographic Software: Zip Zap Map! USA*. Use to help students understand how cities in New York and California grew due to their locations.

Map Skills Objective: Use a map to identify various geographically significant aspects of different urban communities.
Cross-Curricular Connection: Math — Understands/applies the concept of numbers; orders relatively small sets of numbers

Lesson 11
MAP SKILLS
Using a Map and Chart to Find Out Where People Live

Mountains, lakes, and rivers are some of the physical features that can be represented on a map. Population is one of the human features.

A. Look at this map of the United States. Write the names of the following physical features that are shown.

1. Rivers Mississippi, Missouri, Ohio, Columbia, Colorado, Rio Grande

2. Mountains Appalachian Mountains, Rocky Mountains, Cascade Range, Sierra Nevada Mountains

3. Lakes The Great Lakes (Huron, Ontario, Michigan, Erie, Superior); Great Salt Lake

4. Oceans Atlantic Ocean, Pacific Ocean

National Geography Standards: 1, 11, 12
Basic Geography Skills: Analyzing and organizing geographic information and answering geographic questions
Geographic Themes: Human/Environmental Interaction — Relationship within places; Location — Position on Earth's surface

Informal Assessment: As students read the population chart, check to make sure they understand that the cities are arranged alphabetically and that they will rank them in order of population.

B. Read the city names and their populations on the chart.

1. Complete the chart by ranking the cities from 1 to 10 from largest to smallest population.
2. Locate each city on the map.

Population of Large Cities in the United States

City	Population*	Rank
Chicago, IL	2,768,483	3
Dallas, TX	1,022,497	7
Detroit, MI	1,012,110	9
Houston, TX	1,690,180	4
Los Angeles, CA	3,489,779	2
New York, NY	7,311,966	1
Philadelphia, PA	1,552,572	5
Phoenix, AZ	1,012,230	8
San Antonio, TX	966,437	10
San Diego, CA	1,148,851	6

*Population as of July 1, 1992

C. List the cities on the map that are located near each of the following: (Possible answers include the following.)

Rivers Memphis, New Orleans, Omaha, Kansas City, St. Louis, Minneapolis, Cincinnati

Lakes Milwaukee, Chicago, Buffalo, Cleveland, Salt Lake City

Oceans Boston, New York, San Francisco, San Diego, Seattle, Miami, Baltimore, Los Angeles

D. Why do you think so many large cities are located on or near water?

Being near water makes travel and trade easier; products can be easily transported by water; water was a power source.

Activity Objective: Explore an important aspect of an urban community.
Cross-Curricular Connection: Language Arts — Effectively gathers/uses information for research purposes; asks and seeks to answer questions about people/places within (or outside of) the local community
Almanac: See pages 126 and 132–133.

Lesson 11

ACTIVITY Explore an important feature of an urban community.

Investigating a City

The BIG Geographic Question

What makes an urban community a city?

From the article you learned how one city grew to become a big urban area with increased business, transportation, and population. In the map skills lesson you looked at the United States' largest cities that are located near water. Now investigate the human features of your own or a nearby urban community.

A. Listed here are five important features of a city. Describe what each one means. Use the Glossary or Almanac in the back of your book to help you.

1. Population All of the people living in a certain area.

2. Transportation A system for moving passengers and goods from one place to another.

3. Business The occupation, work, or trade in which a person is engaged.

4. Manufacturing Making or producing a product, especially large-scale and by machines.

5. Cultural activities Activities people do to celebrate art, education, or people from different cultures.

National Geography Standards: 9, 10, 11, 12
Basic Geography Skills: Asking and answering geographic questions and analyzing geographic information
Geographic Theme: Human/Environmental Interaction — Relationship within places; Place — Physical and human characteristics

Informal Assessment: Have partners exchange reports and then tell about the information they read.
Standardized Test-Format Assessment: See page 157.

B. Complete the following to find out more about important features of an urban community. (Students' answer will vary according to the urban community they select.)

1. Write the name of the urban community where you live or the one closest to you. (Students' answer will vary according to the urban community they select.)

2. Estimate the population of the city. (Students' answer will vary according to the urban community they select.)

3. Fill in this chart with examples you think describe the city you chose.
(Students' answer will vary according to the urban community they select.)

Features	Examples
Population	
Transportation	
Business	
Manufacturing	
Cultural Activities	

4. Check with a family member, librarian, or encyclopedia to see whether the examples you listed above are correct.

C. Choose one of the features of the city you selected to explore further. Jot down some notes about the feature.

(Students' information will vary depending on the feature they choose to explore.)

D. Design a banner that celebrates and tells something about the community you studied. The banner design should emphasize the feature on which you focused.

(Make sure students' banners include information about the population, housing, stores, transportation routes, businesses, or places for cultural and recreational activities of the city they chose.)

Lesson Overview for pages 68–73: Students study written and graphic materials to learn that suburban communities are geographically important places that developed as a result of movement from rural to urban communities.
Cross-Curricular Connection: History – Understands and knows how to analyze chronological relationships and patterns

Lesson 12

The 'Burbs

As you read about the suburbs, think about how they came to be and why people choose to live there.

When the United States was young, settlers who wanted more land went west. Today when people want more space, they leave the city and move to the **suburbs.** A suburb is a community of homes located at the edge of a city. Almost half of all people in the United States now live in suburbs.

In the 1880s streetcars, and later commuter trains, improved travel out of cities. People could live in towns or villages and travel by trolley or train to and from city jobs.

Since the 1940s roads and highways have become bigger and better. Real estate developers have built large clusters of homes on what was once open land or farmland. Many families have moved into these homes in the suburbs looking for quiet, friendly communities where people know and look out for each other.

Many villages and towns have become the suburbs of a large nearby city.

National Geography Standards: 3, 5, 11, 16
Basic Geography Skills: Acquiring geographic information and answering geographic questions
Geographic Themes: Movement – Humans interacting on Earth; Regions – How they form and change

Informal Assessment: Ask students to discuss the importance of trains, subways, automobiles, and highways in the development of suburbs. They should understand that transportation links suburbs with cities. Within a suburb, transportation links housing developments, offices, stores, and industries.

Families are not the only people moving to the suburbs. Companies locate outside the city, too. Many companies don't want to depend on local materials or markets. They locate near highways, railroad centers, and major airports so they can transport supplies and products to faraway places by truck, train, and plane.

Today more and more people live in one suburb and **commute,** or travel, to another suburb to work. Rarely do these people go to the nearby big city that caused the suburb to grow. When they do, it is usually for entertainment.

Some suburban communities are large tracts of homes that cover big stretches of land away from the city.

Interesting Things to Note

- All cities began as "walking" cities and remained as such until new ways of transportation developed in the late nineteenth century.
- People from farms or small towns move to the suburbs, too. These people usually move to the suburbs to have better access to places like grocery stores, hospitals, and schools.
- Some companies allow workers to "telecommute." These workers avoid traffic by working at home using computers, fax machines, and phone lines to connect to the office.

Living in the suburbs often means spending mornings and evenings on the highways commuting to and from work in the city.

Large interstate highways connect outer suburbs to the city.

Learn More About It: *National Geographic Historical Atlas of the United States*, pp. 240–257; *National Geographic: Exploring Your World*, pp. 101, 337

Map Skills Objective: Use a map to understand geographical terms.
Cross-Curricular Connection: History — Knows how to identify patterns of change and continuity in the history of the community

Lesson 12
MAP SKILLS Using a Map to Understand Geographical Terms

A **metropolitan area** is a large city and its inner and outer suburbs. The city must have a population of 50,000 or more. The inner suburbs are the residential areas closest to a city. The outer suburbs are residential areas that develop as highways extend farther out.

A. Look at the metropolitan area map of Phoenix.

1. Color the city red.
2. Color the inner suburbs blue.
3. Color the outer suburbs green.

(Make sure students have colored the three parts of the map according to the directions.)

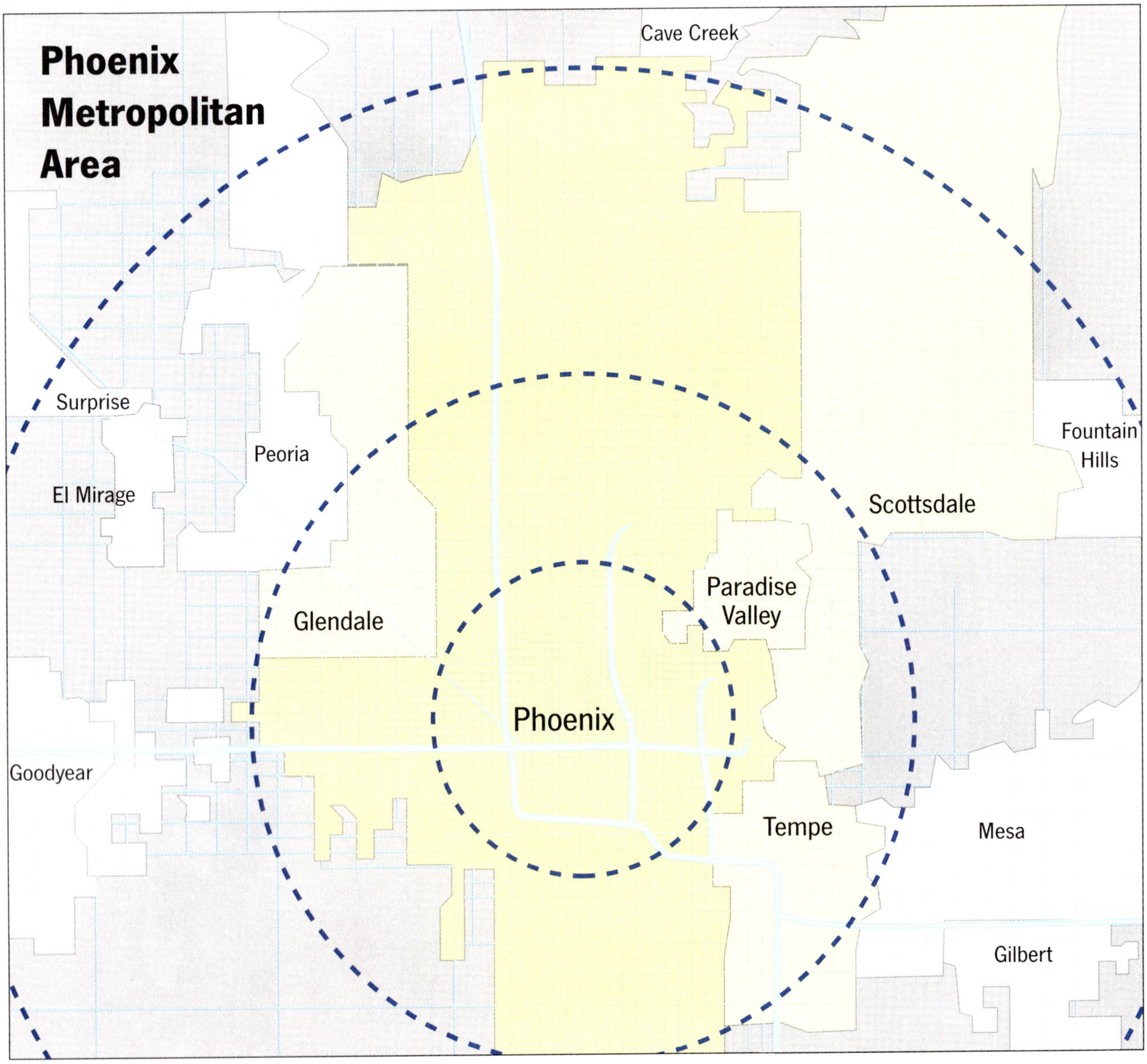

National Geography Standards: 2, 3, 9, 11
Basic Geography Skills: Acquiring and analyzing geographic information
Geographic Themes: Movement — Humans interacting on Earth; Place — Physical and human characteristics

Informal Assessment: Make sure students can use a World Almanac or other source to find the population of the large city they draw. They may come across the term Metropolitan Statistical Area, or MSA, the official term for a metropolitan area. Check to make sure they can use a map of their local area to find names of cities and towns.

B. Complete the following about the area surrounding where you live. (Make sure students correctly identify the area in which they live.)

1. Write the name of the town in which you live. ______________________

2. Write the names of other suburban areas near you. ______________________

______________________ ______________________

3. Write the name of the largest city near you. ______________________

C. Using the map of Phoenix as a model, draw the area in which you live. Include your town, other cities around your town, and the nearest large city. (Students should sketch a map showing the city in relation to where they live.)

D. On the map you drew, circle and label the city, inner suburbs, and outer suburbs of the area in which you live.

Activity Objective: Explore how a nearby suburban community developed.
Cross-Curricular Connection: Language Arts — Effectively gathers/uses information for research purposes; asks and seeks to answer questions about the local community
Almanac: See page 126.

Lesson 12

ACTIVITY Explore how a nearby suburban community developed.

Exploring a Suburb

The BIG Geographic Question

As a suburb develops, how does the area change?

From the article you learned that people leave both the city and the country to live in the suburbs. The map skills lesson helped you look at the area in which you live in relation to suburbs. Now find out how a suburb near you has grown.

A. Write about the area where you live.

(Make sure students are able to describe their community as a city, a rural town, or a suburban town; name surrounding cities and towns; and describe specific means of transportation.)

1. Name the area where you live. ______
2. Is it a city, rural town, or suburb? ______
3. What is a nearby major city? ______
4. What are some nearby suburbs? ______
5. How do people travel between the suburbs and the city or between two suburbs? ______
6. Where do your family members work? ______
7. If they work outside the home, how do they travel to work? ______
8. Where do you go to school? ______
9. How do you get to school? ______
10. Where do you shop? ______
11. Where are the stores, and how do you get to them? ______

National Geography Standards: 3, 9, 14, 17
Basic Geography Skills: Acquiring geographic information and answering geographic questions
Geographic Themes: Human/Environmental Interaction — Relationship within places; Movement — Humans interacting on Earth

Informal Assessment: Encourage students to make a large chart of the features in a community — houses, roads, open land, stores, schools, and transportation. Have them contribute the information they learned about how communities change.
Standardized Test-Format Assessment: See page 158.

B. Think about the houses, roads, open land, stores, schools, and transportation in your suburb or a nearby suburban community. Are they new? Have they always been there? How have they changed? Write some questions you can ask someone to help you find out.

Features	Questions to Ask
Houses	(As students think about the features in their own or a nearby suburban community, they should write specific questions they will ask an adult.)
Roads	
Open Land	
Stores	
Schools	
Transportation	

C. Now interview an older family member, a neighbor, or a school employee. Ask your questions. Take notes on what you learn.

(Make sure students take notes as they conduct their interviews.)

____

____

____

____

____

D. Decide how you will share your information. Then present what you learned about suburbs in your area. (Students should make an oral or written presentation along with a recording, a graphic, or a visual display.)

_______ report

_______ picture time line

_______ photographs, drawings

_______ tape recording

Materials: information about the metropolitan area where you live or near where you live (such as names of inner and outer suburbs, population, and so on)

Lesson 13

From Seed to Sandwich

As you read about the steps involved in making bread, think about how it shows that geography connects people and places.

Bread is a basic food in many parts of the world. It comes in an amazing variety of shapes and sizes. People can make it at home or buy it in a store. Let's look at the geography involved in the process of making bread—from seed to sandwich.

Plant seeds

Wheat grows on farms. Farmers plant spring wheat to harvest in fall and winter wheat to harvest the next spring or summer.

Harvest grain

When wheat is golden brown, it is ready to harvest. Farmers in the Midwest gather their crops by using a combine harvester. This machine is able to cut, thresh, and clean the grain.

Store grain

Trucks transport the wheat to the granary, a place where wheat is stored. Later, trucks take some of the wheat to grain elevators. Some grain is sold to milling companies. They grind the grain into flour.

TRANSPORT

Informal Assessment: Have students demonstrate their understanding of how wheat seeds become bread for sandwiches by summarizing the steps and the places involved in the process.

Enjoy!

The seed that was planted in a farmer's field far away from here has become ready for you to enjoy at your own table.

Food for Thought

The longest loaf of bread on record was 3,491 feet and 9 inches long. It was baked at the Hyatt Regency Hotel in Guadalajara, Mexico, on January 6, 1991.

TRANSPORT

Buy bread

At the store the bread is put on shelves. When it comes to buying bread, people have many choices.

TRANSPORT

Package bread

After the bread cools, it is sliced and wrapped. The wrapped bread travels on big trucks to stores nearby and far away.

TRANSPORT

Make flour

At modern mills the milling process can take up to forty steps. Both white flour and whole wheat flour are made at the mill.

TRANSPORT

Bake bread

The flour is transported to a bakery. There, bakers add water, sugar, milk powder, yeast, vitamins, and minerals to the flour to make bread dough. A commercial bakery can produce many loaves of bread at one time.

Program Resource: *National Geographic Picture Atlas of Our Fifty States*, pp. 160–163; *National Geographic Software: Zip Zap Map! USA*. Use to learn about Nebraska, a wheat-producing state.

Map Skills Objective: Use a map to show the communities through which a product travels as a way to show that communities are connected.
Cross-Curricular Connection: History – Understands the nature of technological design; knows that designing a solution to a simple problem may have constraints such as cost, materials, space, and safety

Lesson 13

MAP SKILLS Using a Road Map to Get from Place to Place

We can use a road map to plan the best route to get where we want to go. The key to a road map can help us tell on what type of road we will be traveling. The map below shows one route that bread travels from seed to sandwich.

A. Look at the map of the Midwest. Circle the following.

1. Langdon, North Dakota
2. Duluth, Minnesota
3. Minneapolis, Minnesota
4. Sioux City, Iowa
5. Elmhurst, Illinois

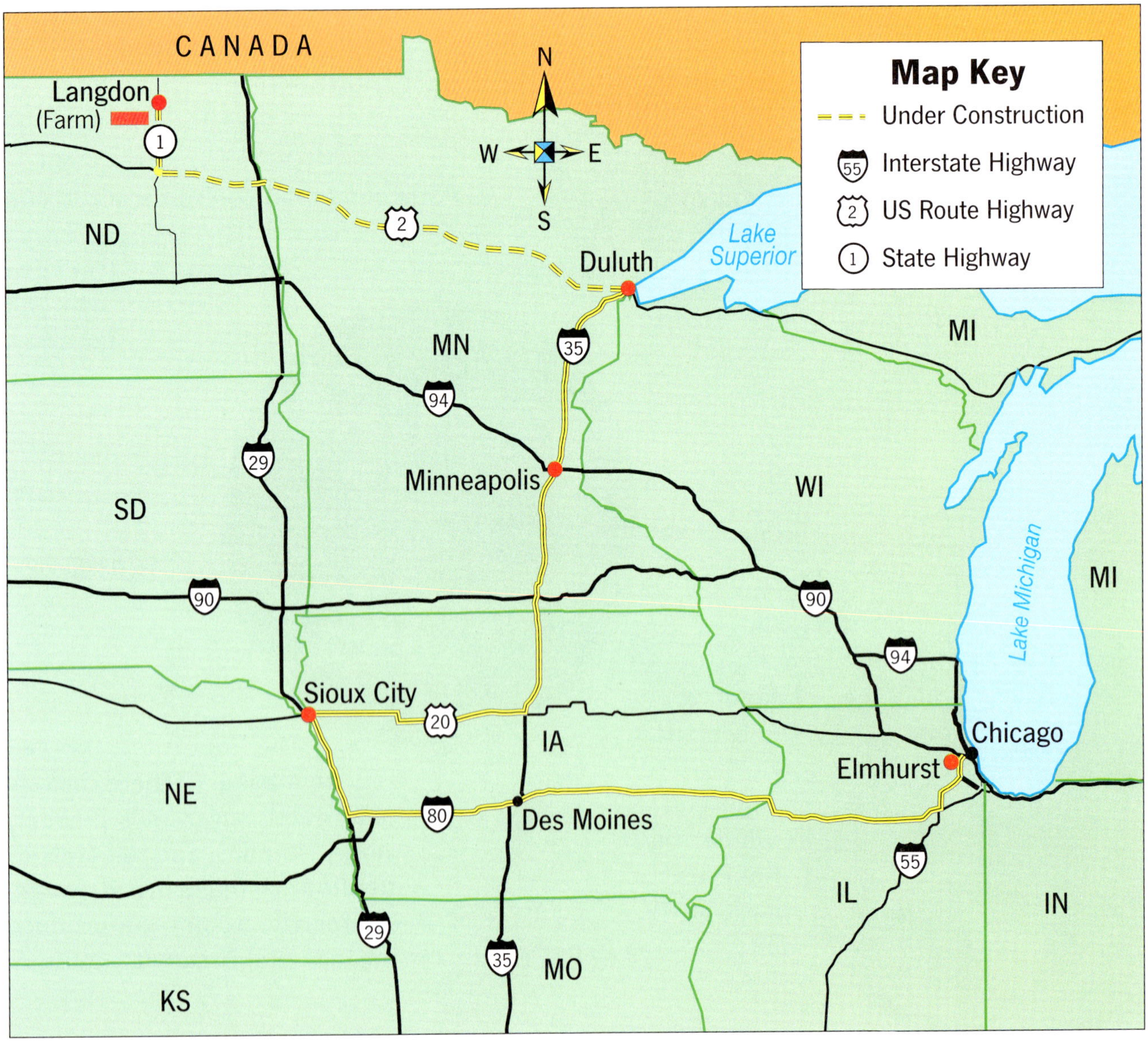

National Geography Standards: 1, 11, 16
Basic Geography Skills: Acquiring and analyzing geographic information and answering geographic questions
Geographic Themes: Location – Position on Earth's surface; Movement – Humans interacting on Earth

Informal Assessment: Check to be sure students understand the key and what the different symbols mean. You might ask students to identify two cities connected by an unpaved road or two cities connected by an interstate highway.

B. Study the map and answer the following.

1. Find the city of Langdon, North Dakota. Grain is harvested on a farm, then loaded onto a truck and taken to Langdon.
   - **a.** What direction will the truck travel to get from Langdon to Highway 2? south
   - **b.** What road will the truck driver take to get from Langdon to Highway 2? Highway 1
2. The grain is stored in Duluth, Minnesota.
   - **a.** What direction will the truck travel to get to Duluth? east or southeast
   - **b.** Trace Highway 2 to Duluth. Why should the truck driver allow extra time? Part of Highway 2 is under construction.
3. The grain is sold to a mill in Minneapolis, Minnesota. There it will be ground into flour.
   - **a.** What direction will the truck travel to get from Duluth to Minneapolis, Minnesota? south
   - **b.** What road will the truck driver use? Highway 35
   - **c.** What does the special symbol around the highway number mean? It means the highway is an interstate.
   - **d.** How would you give directions from Duluth to Minneapolis? Go south on Interstate 35.
4. The flour is sold to a bakery in Sioux City, Iowa. There it will be made into bread. Write directions for getting from Minneapolis to Sioux City, Iowa. Go south on Interstate 35, then west on Highway 20.
5. Write directions for how the packaged bread will travel from the bakery in Sioux City, Iowa, to the grocery store in Elmhurst, Illinois. Go south on Interstate 29, east on Interstate 80, northeast on Interstate 55.

Activity Objective: Plot on a map the communities that are connected by student-selected products.
Cross-Curricular Connection: Science — Understands the nature of technological design; knows that designing a solution to a simple problem may have constraints such as cost, materials, and safety
Almanac: See pages 112–113.

Lesson 13

ACTIVITY

Find out the many places that products you use pass through.

A Link to Other Cities

The BIG Geographic Question

How do products you use connect you to other cities?

From the article you learned the steps it takes to make a loaf of bread. The map skills lesson showed you how people in different places can be connected by the foods they eat. Now find out how the products you use at home connect you to people in other places.

A. Write the names of four products you and your family use.

(Students' answers might include products such as cereal, bread, soap, paper, and so on.)

1. ______________________
2. ______________________
3. ______________________
4. ______________________

B. Read the information on the package for each product and use it to complete the table below. (Students' answers will vary according to products listed above.)

Product Name	City or State of Distributor	Other Cities on Label

National Geography Standards: 1, 11, 16
Basic Geography Skills: Acquiring and analyzing geographic information and answering geographic questions
Geographic Themes: Location — Position on Earth's surface; Movement — Humans interacting on Earth

Informal Assessment: Have students describe how the products they use connect them to people in many places.
Standardized Test-Format Assessment: See page 159.

(Make sure students have correctly identified on the map the cities and states in which products are located.)

C. Look at the city names you listed in the table.

1. Copy each city and state name from your chart onto a small piece of scrap paper. Also include the product name on each piece of paper.
2. Locate a United States map in the Almanac. Find each city on the map. Tape your note on the map next to that city or state.
3. Use yarn or string to connect the cities to your hometown. Use tape to hold the strings in place.
4. Look at the map with your labels in place and answer the following questions.
   a. What product is produced closest to your town?

   ____

   b. What product is produced farthest from your town?

   ____

   c. What city, if any, provides more than one product?

   ____

D. Select one of the products you listed and answer the following questions. (Students' descriptions will vary.)

1. What kind of product is it? Is it a food product, a clothing item, a school supply, etc.? ______________________________

   ____

2. Do you think it is grown on a farm or made in a factory? ______________

   ____

3. Do you think one person grows or makes it in one place or many people grow or help make it in many places? ______________________

   ____

E. Do some further research on your selected product. Check your answers to the questions above and get more information about the product. Use the article as a model to create a step-by-step diagram of how your product is made.

Materials: labels from packages of consumer products so students can find city of distributor, main ingredients, and other product information; yarn or string; map of the United States

Lesson Overview for pages 80–85: Students use written and graphic information to learn that communication and transportation are necessary and important connections between communities.
Cross-Curricular Connection: History – Understands changes in transportation and their effects; understands the travel and communication difficulties encountered by people over vast expanses of territory and the social and economic effects of these developments

Lesson 14

A Race for Life

As you read about how the Iditarod Trail Sled Dog Race started, think about how geography can affect a community.

The Iditarod Trail Sled Dog Race is more than 1,000 miles long. In Alaska's frozen north, racers run through forests, cross mountains and ice, and travel along the coast. The first race, in 1973, took twenty days. Today the racers finish in about ten days. The race is about more than speed. It is about keeping communities connected. It is about remembering others who raced the Iditarod Trail to save lives.

In January 1925, two children in Nome, Alaska, had a deadly disease called diphtheria. The doctor knew many people could die from the disease. He needed a special serum to save everyone. But there was a big problem. He needed to find the serum. Nome was an **isolated** town, meaning it was cut off from other towns in Alaska. It was also winter in Nome. No supplies could come in until the weather got better. Desperate, the doctor asked for help. The mayor sent telegrams to many places, trying to locate the serum. Finally, the serum was found in Anchorage.

Iditarod racers and their dogs brave snow on their trail from Anchorage to Nome.

There was another big problem. How would the serum get from Anchorage to Nome? It could not come by boat. The Bering Sea was frozen. It could not come by plane. At that time, airplanes had open cockpits, and a pilot might freeze to death. The only hope was for the serum to travel by train and dogsled. The journey would be very dangerous.

National Geography Standards: 4, 5, 6
Basic Geography Skills: Acquiring and analyzing geographic information
Geographic Themes: Human/Environmental Interaction – Relationship within places; Movement – Humans interacting on Earth

Informal Assessment: Have students demonstrate their understanding by identifying problems and solutions from the 1925 race along the Iditarod Trail. Their answers might look like these:

Problems:	Sick children	Winter in Nome; no supplies	Sea frozen; too cold for planes	Long distance, dangerous, cold, blizzards
Solutions:	Get serum	Send telegrams for help	Use train and dogsled trail	Use relay teams to keep the serum moving day and night

Dogsled relay teams met along the Iditarod Trail. The drivers and their dogs faced challenges. Racing day and night, they battled blizzards. They fought temperatures far below zero. They faced hungry, wild animals. Once, the serum was almost lost when it fell off the sled.

Despite these problems, the teams completed the journey in five days! The people of Nome were saved. Today the 1,159-mile Iditarod race is the toughest race in the world. Every year people come to test their skills and to remember the brave people and dogs who completed the first race for life.

Program Resource: *National Geographic CD-ROM: Picture Atlas of the World; National Geographic Software: Zip Zap Map! USA.* Use to view the terrain of Alaska.

Map Skills Objective: Use a map to identify the equator, prime meridian, and the hemispheres.
Cross-Curricular Connection: Math — Understands the general nature/uses of mathematics; understands that numbers can be used to describe things in the real world

Lesson 14 Map Skills

Using the Equator and Prime Meridian to Identify Hemispheres

Maps show imaginary lines that can help us explain where places are located. One line is the **equator**. It goes around Earth's center. It divides the world into the northern and the southern hemispheres. Another line is the **prime meridian.** It goes around Earth from top to bottom. It divides the world into the western and the eastern hemispheres.

A. Look at the world maps below. Circle the following terms.

1. Equator
2. Prime Meridian
3. Northern Hemisphere
4. Southern Hemisphere
5. Western Hemisphere
6. Eastern Hemisphere

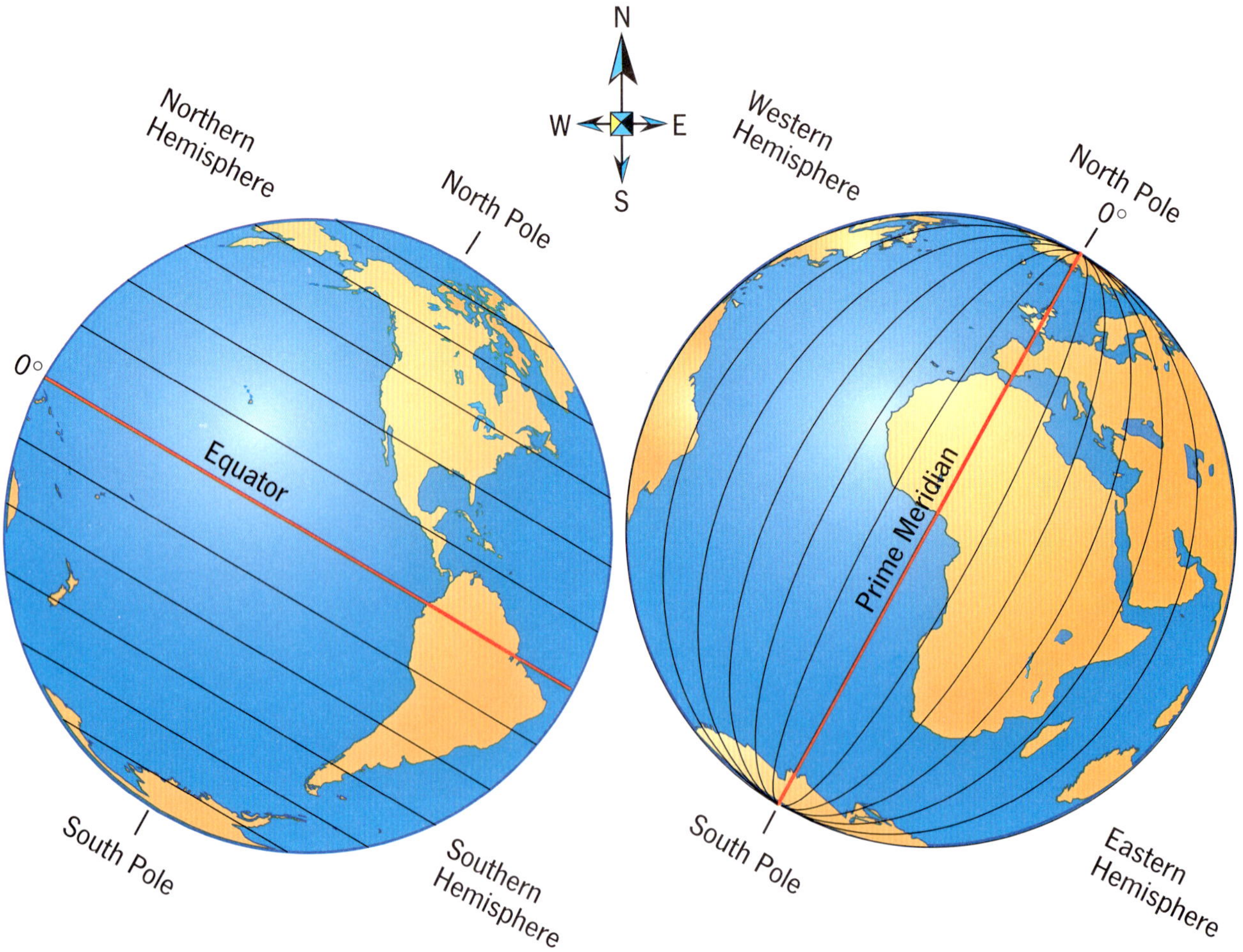

National Geography Standards: 1, 4, 5
Basic Geography Skills: Asking and answering geographic questions
Geographic Theme: Location — Position on Earth's surface

Informal Assessment: Check to make sure students can identify hemispheres by asking them to tell in which hemispheres different countries or continents are located.

B. Look at the map with the equator labeled.

1. In what direction would you move your finger to trace the equator?

   east and west

2. What is the half of Earth north of the equator called?

   northern hemisphere

3. What is the half of Earth south of the equator called?

   southern hemisphere

4. Is the Iditarod Trail in the northern hemisphere or the southern hemisphere?

   northern hemisphere

C. Look at the map with the prime meridian labeled.

1. In what direction would you move your finger to trace the prime meridian? north and south

2. What is the half of Earth to the west of the prime meridian called?

   western hemisphere

3. What is the half of Earth to the east of the prime meridian called?

   eastern hemisphere

4. Is the Iditarod Trail in the western hemisphere or the eastern hemisphere?

   western hemisphere

D. Find the continent and country of your home state on one of the maps.

1. Is your home state in the northern or southern hemisphere?

   northern hemisphere

2. Is it in the western or eastern hemisphere? western hemisphere

3. Which is closer to the equator, your home state or Alaska?

   the students' home state, unless home state is Alaska, then answer should be "same"

Activity Objective: Identify isolated communities that realized the importance of being connected to other communities.
Cross-Curricular Connection: Language Arts – Effectively gathers/uses information for research purposes; uses encyclopedias and dictionaries to gather information
Almanac: See page 125.

Lesson 14

ACTIVITY

Find out where other isolated communities are located.

Community Connections

The BIG Geographic Question

Why do isolated communities need to stay connected with other communities?

From the article you learned about the Iditarod Trail Sled Dog Race, and how the Iditarod Trail connected an isolated community with other places. The map skills lesson showed you how to locate communities on a part of the globe. Now you will find out about other isolated communities and how they connect with other people and places.

A. Circle one of these isolated communities to read about.

1. Buffalo, New York, in the 1800s
2. Salt Lake City, Utah, in the 1800s

(Students' selections will vary, however you may wish to group together students who make like selections.)

B. Answer as many of the following questions as you can about the isolated community you selected. Look in the Almanac for help with answering these questions.

(Check students' answers against information in the Almanac about Buffalo and Salt Lake City.)

1. Why did people settle there? ____________________
2. Why was it isolated? ____________________
3. Why might the community need to be in touch with other communities?

____

4. Did any specific event make that community build a connection with other communities? ____________________

____

National Geography Standards: 1, 4, 5, 6
Basic Geography Skills: Acquiring and analyzing geographic information
Geographic Themes: Human/Environmental Interaction – Relationship within places; Location – Position on Earth's surface

Informal Assessment: Have students name the community they read about and find it on a map. Then ask them to point out physical characteristics on the map that contributed to that community's isolation.
Standardized Test-Format Assessment: See page 160.

C. Answer the following questions, then discuss them with a classmate.

1. How do you think people decide where to build communities? (Possible answers include: near water, roads, or a major transportation route so they can transport goods or where there is good soil to farm. People may also build communities in a certain place for religious or political reasons.)

2. What physical features might isolate a community? (Possible answers include: mountains that are hard to cross, poor soil, extreme heat or cold, or being a great distance from other communities.)

3. Why do you think people in communities need to be in touch with others? (Possible answers include: to communicate with one another, to help each other in emergencies, and to supply each other with needed goods and services.)

4. How might people in an isolated community connect with other communities? (Possible answers include: They could communicate by mail, telegraph, telephone, fax, or computer. They could also travel by bus, train, car, plane, or boat to visit one another.)

D. Now create a collage that represents the isolated community you selected to learn about. You may draw, cut out, or paint pictures and paste them on your collage. It should help viewers understand how the community was isolated and how it later became connected to other communities. Share your collage with the class and compare it with your classmates' collages.

(Students' collages should show some understanding of the physical features—geography—that isolated their selected community and how that geographical challenge was overcome to connect the community with other ones.)

Lesson Overview for pages 86–91: Students use written and graphic materials to understand that over time, the need to overcome geographical obstacles has led to advancements in communication and transportation technologies and new ways of doing things.
Cross-Curricular Connection: History — Understands changes in communication and their effects; knows ways people communicate with each other now and long ago and the technological developments that facilitated communication

Lesson 15

WHAT'S THE CONNECTION?

As you read about the advances in transportation and communication, think about the role geography played in these advances through time.

There was a time when it took days, weeks, and even months for people to travel between communities. Today we can fly across the country in less than a day. We can send and receive news within seconds. What changes have made this possible? What geographical obstacles had to be overcome?

Hundreds of years ago, Native Americans traveled by foot or water. When they needed to send messages long distances, they sent smoke signals or used drums. The early colonists traveled on foot, by water, or on horseback. It wasn't until much later that roads were cut through thick forests, and stagecoaches carried passengers between cities and towns.

foot travel

CHANGES IN TRANSPORTATION

covered wagon

paddle wheel steamers

train

zeppelin

National Geography Standards: 6, 17, 18
Basic Geography Skills: Asking and answering geographic questions
Geographic Theme: Regions — How they form and change

Informal Assessment: Have pairs of students demonstrate their understanding by playing "Twenty Questions" about a means of transportation or communication. Encourage students to include questions about geographical obstacles that needed to be overcome.

With the invention of trains in the mid-1800s, overland travel became even easier. Mountains were no longer an obstacle because railroad tracks could be made to go over, around, and through them. By the 1920s cars became the chief means of transportation in the United States. In the 1950s airplanes made travel even faster.

Changes in Communication

Pony Express

telegraph

telephone

radio

A Blast from the Past

You already know what a car, subway, plane, and computer look like. Check out these images of transportation methods and communication tools from the past.

New ways of communicating have changed the way people live and do things, too. Centuries ago, news traveled only as fast as people did–on foot, horseback, or ship. Messages were sent across land by stagecoach and the Pony Express over a period of days or weeks. When a system of telegraph wires was connected across the country, messages could be sent in minutes.

The invention of the telephone improved communication even further in the late 1800s. Radio and television, which did not need wires to send messages, came along later and changed communication even more. Today millions of computers are connected by the Internet, an information "superhighway" used for sending and receiving information instantly using telephone lines.

Learn More About It: *National Geographic Historical Atlas of the United States,* pp. 182–203

Map Skills Objective: Use a map to communicate how, over time, developments in transportation and communication have led to covering more distance in less time.
Cross-Curricular Connection: Math – Effectively uses a variety of strategies in the problem-solving process; solves real-world problems involving addition and subtraction of numbers

Lesson 15
MAP SKILLS
Using a Map to Figure Travel Time

Maps can be used to show the different methods used to send messages from one place to another. The map's key can help identify the different routes and the time each took.

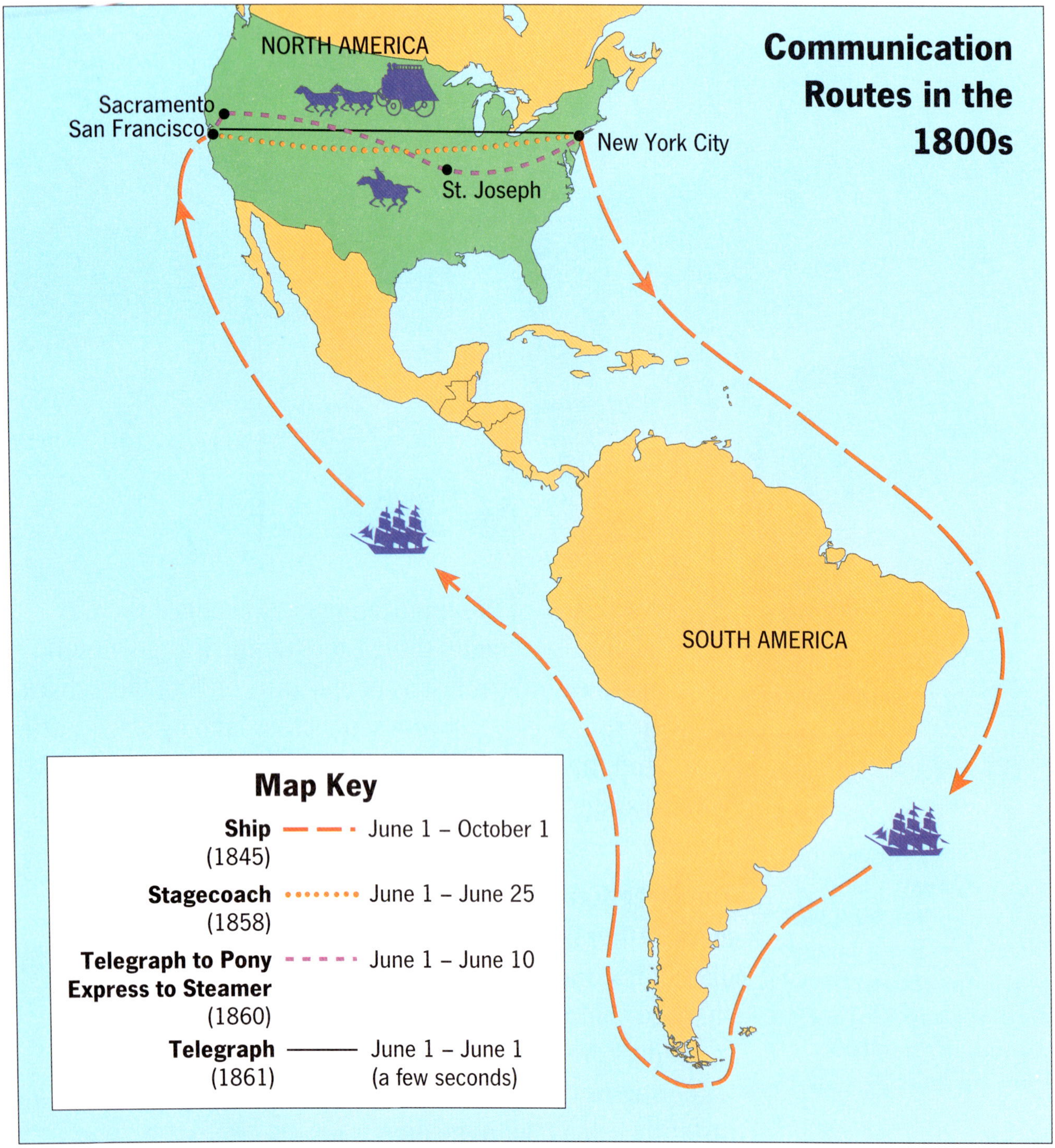

National Geography Standards: 1, 11, 17
Basic Geography Skills: Acquiring, analyzing, and organizing geographic information
Geographic Theme: Movement – Humans interacting on Earth

Informal Assessment: Challenge students to create and solve their own word problems that involve "start" and "end" dates or comparisons of the times involved.

A. Look at the map and answer the following questions.

1. What color and symbol show the route of the stagecoach? orange • • • • • •

2. What color and symbol show the route of the ship? red — — — —

B. Answer the following questions about each route on the map.

1. Look at the stagecoach route.
   a. What is the starting date? June 1
   b. When did it get to San Francisco? June 25
   c. How long did it take the stagecoach to deliver the message from New York to San Francisco? 24 or 25 days

2. Look at the ship route.
   a. What is the starting date? June 1
   b. When did the ship get to San Francisco? October 1
   c. How long did it take the ship to deliver the message? 4 months

3. Looking at the message route in 1860, answer the following questions.
   a. What three methods were used to send a message?

      telegraph | pony express | steamer

   b. How long did it take to deliver the message during the 1860 trip using these three methods? 9 or 10 days
   c. What was the time difference between how long it took in 1858 and in 1860? 15 days

4. Find the delivery method that was fastest.
   a. How was it sent and in what year was the method used?

      telegraph; 1861

   b. How long did it take? a few seconds

Activity Objective: Show on a graph the difference in time required to send a message from one place to another during different periods in history.
Cross-Curricular Connection: Math — Understands/applies concepts of data analysis and distributions; constructs simple bar graphs
Almanac: See pages 132–133.

Lesson 15

ACTIVITY

Show the time it takes to send messages in different ways.

Message Express!

The BIG Geographic Question

What effect did geography have on the amount of time it took to send messages in the mid-1800s?

The article helped you understand how methods of communication and transportation changed over time. The map skills lesson showed you that developments in communication shortened the time needed to send messages. Now make a graph to show what you have learned.

A. List some ways of sending messages that you learned about in the article on pages 86–87.

1. computers
2. Pony Express
3. radio
4. smoke signals
5. stagecoach
6. telegraph
7. telephone
8. television

B. List the ways that were shown in the map skills lesson.

1. Pony Express
2. ship
3. stagecoach
4. steamer
5. telegraph

National Geography Standard: 6, 11, 17
Basic Geography Skills: Acquiring, organizing, and analyzing geographic information
Geographic Theme: Movement — Humans interacting on Earth

Informal Assessment: Have students compare their charts with their graphs to make sure the information is consistent. Encourage them to look for any discrepancies.
Standardized Test-Format Assessment: See page 161.

C. Use what you've learned to fill in the chart.

Year	Type of Communication	Approximate Time to Deliver Message
1845	ship	4 months
1858	overland stagecoach	25 days
1860	telegraph, pony express, steamer	10 days
1861	telegraph	few seconds

D. Organize your information on a graph. Show the difference in time required to send a message from New York City to San Francisco at different points in time.

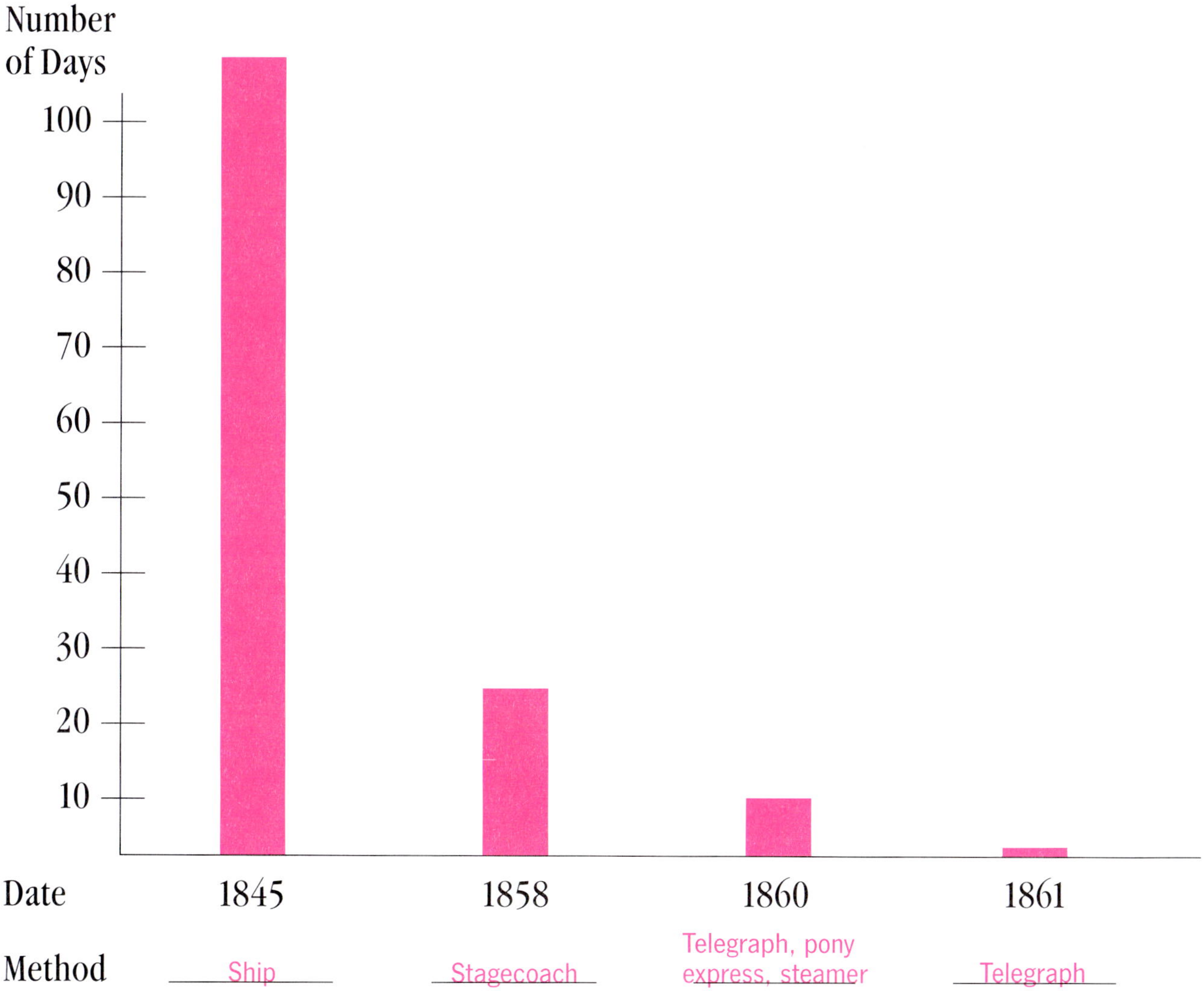

Lesson 16

From "Ghost Town" to "Ski Town"

As you read about Telluride, think about how geography has changed the community over time.

Telluride, Colorado, is located high in the Rocky Mountains on the banks of the San Miguel River. It lies at the end of a **box canyon,** a valley so steep its walls seem almost vertical. Geography has played a key role in Telluride's history.

For years the town was called Columbia. Then, in 1875, silver and gold were discovered. People rushed there to mine the ore. The town was renamed Telluride in 1881 after a miner there found a metal called tellurium, which he thought was valuable.

Telluride turned out to be a town rich in natural resources, but it was isolated. Moving ore to mills in other towns was difficult and costly. By the end of the 1880s the mining stopped.

People left in the late 1880s, and Telluride became a ghost town.

Informal Assessment: Have students demonstrate their understanding by making a time line of Telluride's history. Their time line might look like this:

1875	1890	1914	1953	1996
• isolated • silver & gold mines	• railroad • 4,000 people	• major flood • 500 people • business destroyed	• mines reopen	• ski area • 1,300 residents

The railroad connected Telluride to the outside world.

In 1890 the Rio Grande Southern Railroad reached Telluride. The ore could be transported to mills. The miners returned, and the town prospered. Its population rose to 4,000.

In 1914 a flood destroyed homes and businesses. By 1930, at the time of the Great Depression, the bank and most mines closed. The population fell again, this time to about 500.

In 1953 the Idarado Mining Company bought the mines. Telluride was revived as it mined millions of dollars worth of copper, lead, zinc, silver, and gold. In 1978 the ores ran out, and the Idarado Mining Company closed.

The mines no longer support the people of Telluride. Still, the community is thriving. The winter snow in the high mountains attracts skiers. In fall the mountains and the surrounding national forest draw many hikers to the area.

People come to Telluride by car or plane. Some are rowed down the San Miguel River in a gondola. The lofty peaks, once an obstacle, are now the main attraction for Telluride's 1,300 residents and its many visitors.

Skiers enjoy the snowy slopes of the Telluride ski area.

Program Resource: *National Geographic Picture Atlas of Our Fifty States,* pp. 216–217. Use to read about the physical features of Colorado and how they affect the state's economy.

Map Skills Objective: Locate places and features on a map, and use a map scale to figure out the distance from one place to another.
Cross-Curricular Connection: Math — Understands and applies the concept of measurement

Lesson 16

Map Skills Using a Map Scale to Figure Out Distance

Maps can show how far places are from each other. We can use a map scale to figure this out. On this map scale, one inch on a ruler would equal fifty miles on the map.

A. Look at the map of Colorado below. Circle the following items.

1. Telluride
2. Denver (capital of Colorado)
3. Roads leading to Telluride
4. Rivers near Telluride
5. Elevation of mountains near Telluride
6. The Rocky Mountains

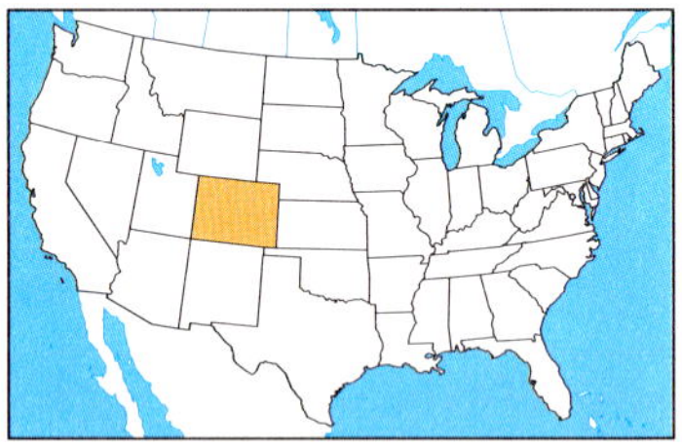

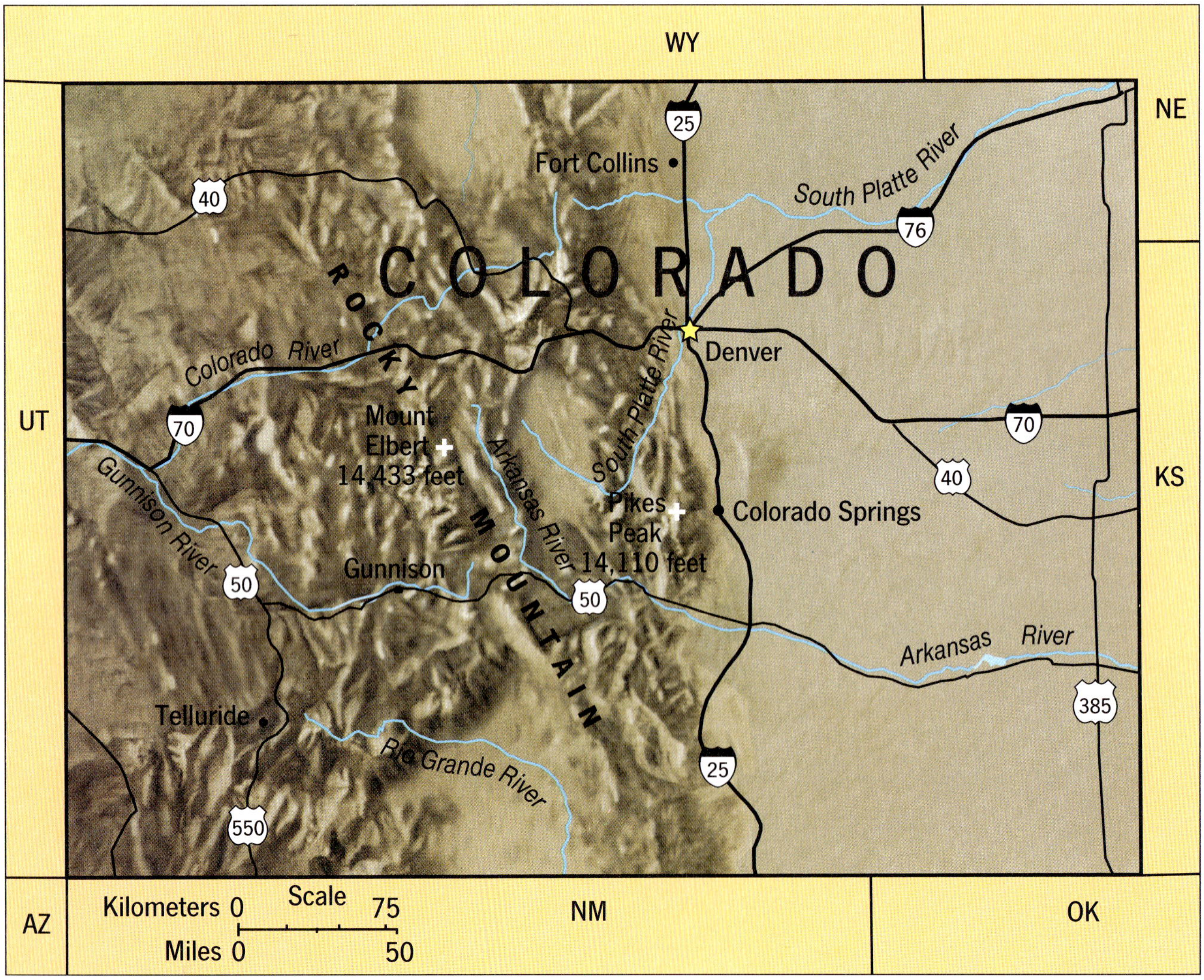

National Geography Standards: 1, 3
Basic Geography Skills: Acquiring geographic information and answering geographic questions
Geographic Theme: Location — Position on Earth's surface

Informal Assessment: Check to make sure students understand how they can use a string to measure curvy road and river routes accurately.

B. Find the distance between Telluride and Denver in air miles, or "as the crow flies."

1. With a ruler, measure the number of inches between Telluride and Denver on the map. Write the number of inches below.

   3.5 inches

2. Use the map scale to find out the following.

   One inch stands for 50 miles.

3. Write down and multiply the numbers in questions 1 and 2 to find out the distance in miles.

   3.5 x 50 = 175

4. On the map, Telluride is approximately 175 miles from Denver by air.

C. Road and river routes are often curvy, so they take a little more time to figure out.

1. Take a piece of string and bend it along a road route from Denver to Telluride.
2. Mark the string at Denver, then straighten it out.
3. Measure the string up to the mark. Write the number of inches below.

   6 inches

4. Write down and multiply the number of inches of string by the number of miles an inch stands for.

   6 x 50 = 300

5. Telluride is approximately 300 miles from Denver by car.
6. Write the directions for the road route you measured from Telluride to Denver. Be sure to include a description of any mountains or rivers you would cross.

   (Possible answers: Take Interstate 25 south past Pikes Peak. Go west on State Route 50, through the Rocky Mountains and across the Arkansas River. Then take State Route 550 south to Telluride.)

Materials: string, ruler

Activity Objective: Explore how one's own community has changed over time.
Cross-Curricular Connection: History — Understands the history of the local community
Almanac: See page 125.

Lesson 16

ACTIVITY

Find out why your community was settled where it is.

Your Community: Then and Now

The BIG Geographic Question

Where and why was your community first settled, and how has it changed over time?

From the article you learned why the community of Telluride was settled where it is and how it changed over time. The map skills lesson showed you how to use a map scale. Now find out how your community was settled and how it has changed.

A. What are two key physical features of your community?
(Make sure students accurately list physical features about their communities.)

1. ______________________________

2. ______________________________

B. Answer as many of the following questions about your community as you can. (Help students find resources to help them answer these questions about their communities.)

1. When was your community settled? ______________________________

____

2. Who settled it? ______________________________

____

3. Why did they settle there? ______________________________

____

____

4. Where does your community get its water? ______________________________

____

National Geography Standards: 4, 12, 17
Basic Geography Skills: Asking and answering geographic questions and acquiring geographic information
Geographic Themes: Place — Physical and human characteristics; Regions — How they form and change

Informal Assessment: Have students compare and contrast their answers to the questions and community models and discuss any discrepancies.
Standardized Test-Format Assessment: See page 162.

C. What do you think your community was like when it was first settled? What is it like now? Write an *M* for *more,* an *L* for *less,* or *S* for *same* for the items listed in the chart.

(Make sure students' answers reflect the characteristics of their communities.)

	Before	Now
open land		
trees		
houses		
roads		
rivers, lakes, or creeks		
farms		
factories		

D. Talk to your friends and family. Go to the library. Find out whether your answers are correct! Then think about what your community is like now. How has it changed? Use the information to draw a picture or make a map of what your community was like when people first settled there and what it is like now.

(Make sure students' pictures or maps reflect characteristics of their communities.)

Before	Now

Materials: rulers, information about your local community (such as physical features, when the community was settled and by whom, why settlers came, and where the community gets its water), art supplies to make model of community

Lesson Overview for pages 98–103: Students study written and graphic materials to learn that human actions can modify the geography of a place.
Cross-Curricular Connection: Science — Understands the interactions of science, technology, and society; knows that the effects of science may be positive or negative

Lesson 17

HOUSTON'S HORIZON

As you read about Houston, think about how the actions of humans affected its geography and the type of city it is.

When Houston, Texas, was first settled in 1836, it was a dusty little town 50 miles from the port city of Galveston. By 1990 it was the fourth largest U.S. city and our nation's third busiest port.

Houston was settled along Buffalo Bayou, which led to the Gulf of Mexico. The **bayou,** a creek or minor river, wasn't deep enough or wide enough for ships to use. This made it difficult for the people of Houston to travel to or to get goods from other places.

In the 1830s many farmers in Texas grew cotton. They needed a way to get their cotton to the port at Galveston to be shipped out. It wasn't until the 1850s, when railroad lines were built, that farmers were able to send their cotton from smaller towns to Houston by rail. It was then sent by barge along the Buffalo Bayou to Galveston. The railroad made it much easier for goods and people to get in and out of Houston.

Today skyscrapers line the streets of downtown Houston.

National Geography Standards: 11, 14, 15, 17
Basic Geography Skills: Acquiring, organizing, and analyzing geographic information
Geographic Theme: Human/Environmental Interaction – Relationship within places

Informal Assessment: Have students demonstrate their understanding by naming the most important geographic change to Houston and by explaining its effects on the city. (The formation of the Houston Ship Channel turned Houston into the third busiest port in the U.S. and helped Houston grow into the fourth largest U.S. city.)

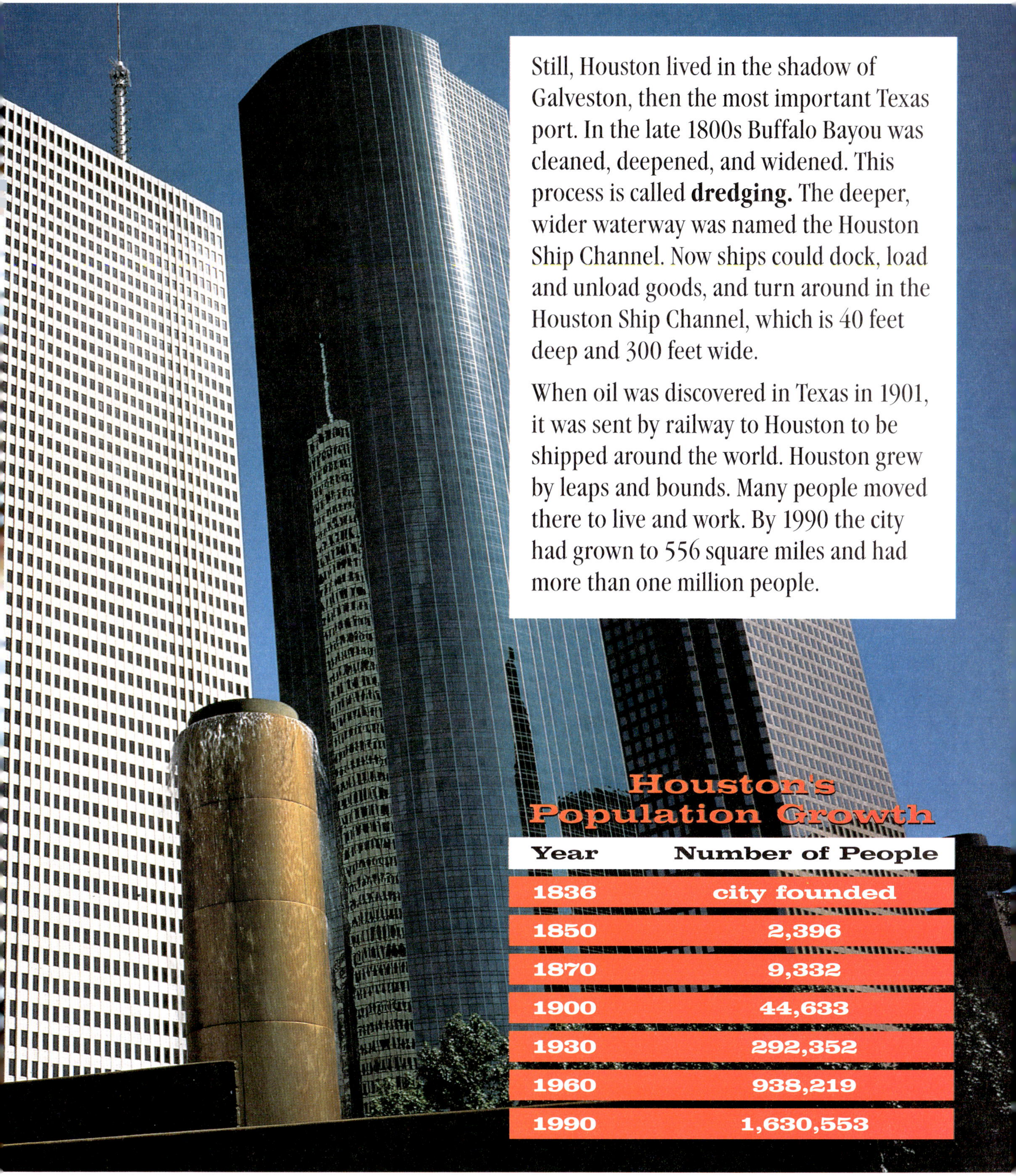

Still, Houston lived in the shadow of Galveston, then the most important Texas port. In the late 1800s Buffalo Bayou was cleaned, deepened, and widened. This process is called **dredging.** The deeper, wider waterway was named the Houston Ship Channel. Now ships could dock, load and unload goods, and turn around in the Houston Ship Channel, which is 40 feet deep and 300 feet wide.

When oil was discovered in Texas in 1901, it was sent by railway to Houston to be shipped around the world. Houston grew by leaps and bounds. Many people moved there to live and work. By 1990 the city had grown to 556 square miles and had more than one million people.

Houston's Population Growth

Year	Number of People
1836	city founded
1850	2,396
1870	9,332
1900	44,633
1930	292,352
1960	938,219
1990	1,630,553

Program Resource: *National Geographic Picture Atlas of Our Fifty States*, pp. 190–191; *National Geographic Software: Zip Zap Map! USA.* Use to learn more about the growth of cities in Texas.
Learn More About It: *National Geographic: Exploring Your World*, pp. 240–241

Map Skills Objective: Use a physical map to locate a city and identify land and water features near the city.
Cross-Curricular Connection: Language Arts — Effectively gathers/uses information for research; uses key words, indexes, cross-references, and letters on volumes to find information for research

Lesson 17

MAP SKILLS

Using a Map to Identify the Water Features of an Area

Maps can show the land and water features of an area. Land features include mountains, plains, and deserts. Water features include rivers, lakes, and oceans.

National Geography Standards: 1, 8, 14
Basic Geography Skills: Acquiring and analyzing geographic information
Geographic Themes: Location — Position on Earth's surface; Place — Physical and human characteristics

Informal Assessment: Check to make sure students can identify the land and water features near each city.

A. Look at the map of Texas. Circle the following.

1. Houston
2. Dallas
3. Rio Grande
4. Galveston
5. Pecos River
6. Gulf of Mexico

B. Use the map to complete the following.

1. Look at the map key. Draw or write the name of the symbol or color that stands for each thing listed.

   a. The symbol for a river is ~ or wavy blue line.

   b. The symbol for a city is • or black dot.

   c. The color that stands for the Great Plains region is orange.

2. What is the capital of Texas? Austin

3. Find Austin on the map. On what river is Austin located?

   Colorado River

4. What river runs between Texas and Mexico?

   Rio Grande

5. What city is located on the Rio Grande?

   El Paso

6. Which city is located closest to the Gulf of Mexico?

   Galveston or Houston

7. Why is it good for a city to be located on or near a river?

   (Possible answers include: it is a source of drinking water, or it can be used to transport goods.)

Activity Objective: Compare one's own community to another community in terms of human modifications.
Cross-Curricular Connection: History — Understands the history of the local community; knows the history of the local community since its founding
Almanac: See page 130.

Lesson 17

ACTIVITY

Find out the source of land and water features in your community.

Your Community's Land and Water

The BIG Geographic Question

Which land and water features in your community are natural?

From the article you learned about the land and water features that helped Houston grow from a small town to the fourth largest city in the United States. In the map skills lesson you used a map to identify important waterways located in Texas. Now find out about land and water features in and around your community.

A. Most land and water features are natural, or made by nature. However, some are artificial, or built by people. Circle each artificial feature listed below.

river	dam	airport	forest
highway	mountain	canal	bridge
ocean	school	railroad	island

B. Complete the following items with information about your community.

1. List the most important land features of your community. (Make sure the features students list can likely be found in their community.)

_______________ _______________

_______________ _______________

_______________ _______________

2. Put an *N* beside the above features that are *natural* and an *A* beside the ones that are *artificial*. (Make sure students have correctly identified the features they listed as natural or artificial.)

National Geography Standards: 1, 3, 14
Basic Geography Skills: Analyzing geographic information and answering geographic questions
Geographic Themes: Location — Position on Earth's surface; Place — Physical and human characteristics

Informal Assessment: Have students compare and contrast their answers to the questions and discuss any discrepancies.
Standardized Test-Format Assessment: See page 163.

3. List the most important water features of your community. (Make sure the features students list can likely be found in their community.)

_______________ _______________

_______________ _______________

_______________ _______________

4. Put an *N* beside the above features that are *natural* and an ***A*** beside the ones that are *artificial.* (Make sure students have correctly identified the features they listed as natural or artificial.)

C. Using the chart below, place a check mark in the box that shows each land and water feature found in your community and each found in Houston. (Make sure students checks below reflect the features found in their community and in Houston.)

Land and Water Features	Your Community	Houston
lake		
river		✓
harbor		✓
mountain		
forest		
highway		✓
bridge		✓
airport		✓
railroad		✓

D. Compare your community with Houston. Think about how artificial features changed Houston. Then think about artificial features that have changed your community. Write a paragraph explaining whether you think the artifical features were a good or bad change for your community. (Students' answers should reflect an understanding of artificial features and how they can change the geography of a community.)

Materials: information about your local community (such as land and water features)

Lesson Overview for pages 104–109: Students use written and graphic materials to learn that geographical formations of some communities are natural wonders.
Cross-Curricular Connection: Science – Understands basic Earth processes; knows that the surface of Earth changes due to slow (erosion, weathering) and rapid (volcanoes, landslides) processes

Lesson 18

Islands of Fire and Rain

As you read about Hawaii, think about how its geography affects where and how people live on the islands.

Being an island really sets a place apart! Hawaii, with its active volcanoes, black beaches, and rain shadows, is very different from the mainland states.

The state of Hawaii is actually made up of eight islands. The largest of the eight islands is Hawaii. People call it the "Big Island." Like the other Hawaiian Islands, Hawaii is really the top of a huge underwater mountain created by the buildup of lava over three million years. The lava hardened and rose above the water level in the Pacific Ocean.

Spitting rocks and fire, Kilauea's fiery lava flows to the sea.

The "Big Island" still has two active volcanoes–Mauna Loa and Kilauea. Their lava has added more than 70 acres of land to Hawaii in the last ten years. Kilauea, the world's most active volcano, erupts every few months.

The climate on each side of Hawaii's high mountains can be very different. For example, Hilo, which is located on the east side of the "Big Island" is very wet. Kailua-Kona, located on the west side, is very dry. The reason for this is a process called **rain shadow.** Cool winds from the east side of the island produce rain that falls into the mountains. As the moisture clouds rise up the mountainside, they become drier. By the time they reach the west side of the mountains, they are dry.

National Geography Standards: 4, 7, 15
Basic Geography Skills: Asking and answering geographic questions
Geographic Themes: Human/Environmental Interaction – Relationship within places; Place – Physical and human characteristics

Informal Assessment: Have students name islands they know of and list the facts they know about islands in general. For example, an island is surrounded by water. Some islands are high; some are low. Some are small; some are huge masses, like Greenland.

The east side of the mountains get more than 200 inches of rain each year. Farmers can grow sugar, macadamia nuts, and flowers in this area. Also, more people live on the east side of the island. However, most of the island's hotels and resorts are on the west side.

In the Hawaiian islands, the sun shines for up to 344 days a year, providing warm temperatures all year. In addition, its location near the equator and cool winds off the Pacific Ocean help keep the temperatures pleasant. Hawaii's beautiful weather and its many stunning sites make it a popular vacation spot.

The "Big Island" boasts beautiful mountains, valleys, cliffs, beaches, and waterfalls.

Wet ocean winds from the east cool and drop their moisture as rain in the mountains. The dry winds rush over the mountains, forming a "rain shadow" and leaving the west with little or no rain.

Map Skills Objective: Use a map to identify the location of the island of Hawaii in relation to the mainland United States.
Cross-Curricular Connection: Language Arts — Effectively gathers/uses information for research; uses key words, indexes, cross-references, and letters on volumes to find information for research

Lesson 18
MAP SKILLS Using Maps to Locate Places Using Directions

The large map below shows the eight major islands that make up the state of Hawaii. The small map is a locator map. It shows where Hawaii is in relation to the rest of the United States. The rest of the United States, which is one big piece of land, is called the "**mainland.**"

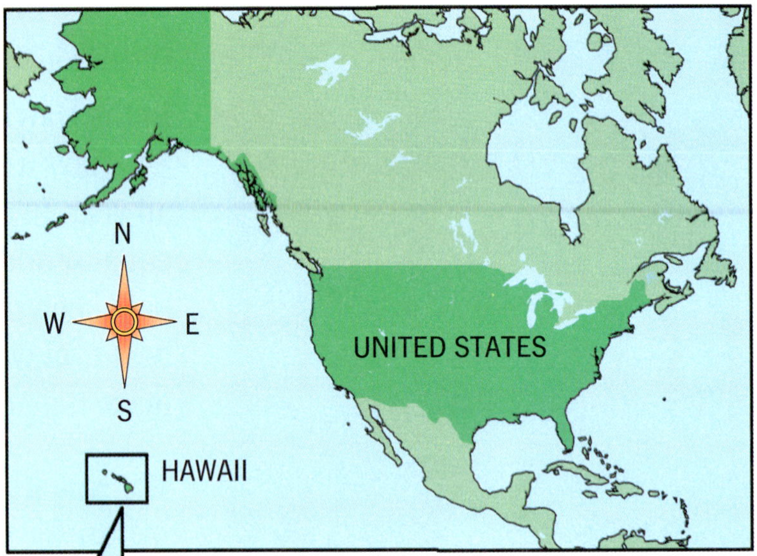

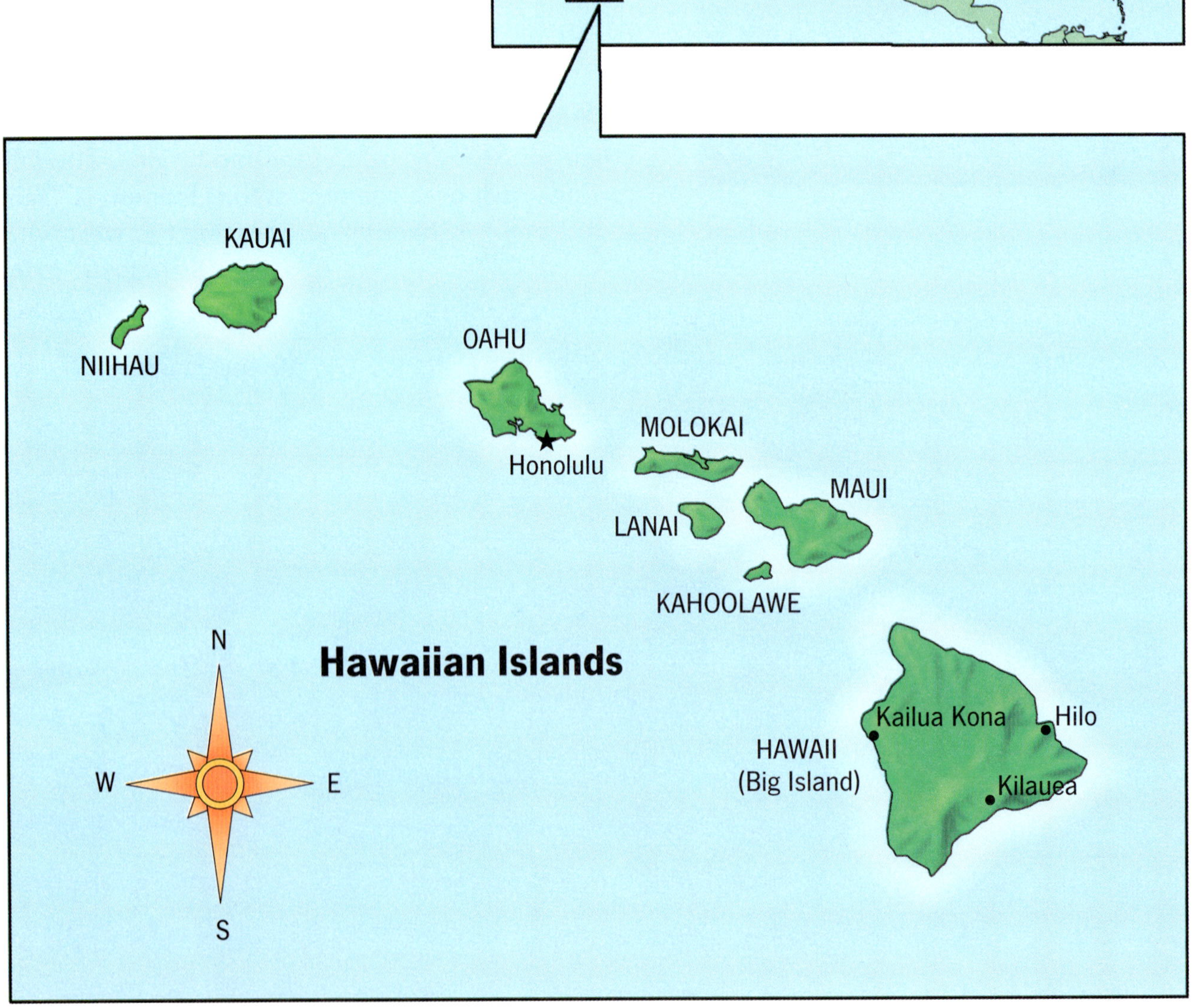

National Geography Standards: 1, 3
Basic Geography Skills: Asking and answering geographic questions
Geographic Theme: Location — Position on Earth's surface

Informal Assessment: Have students use the map scale to determine Hawaii's approximate distance from the United States mainland (2,400 miles). Ask students to identify the southernmost state of the United States mainland (Florida—some students may also say Texas).

A. Look at the main map of Hawaii. Find and number the following places:

1. the "Big Island" Hawaii
2. Hilo
3. Kailua-Kona
4. Kilauea
5. the island of Oahu
6. the island of Maui

B. The compass rose usually shows only the cardinal directions—north, south, east, and west. Sometimes locations are between these four directions. Northeast, northwest, southeast, and southwest are intermediate directions. Fill in all eight directions on the compass rose below.

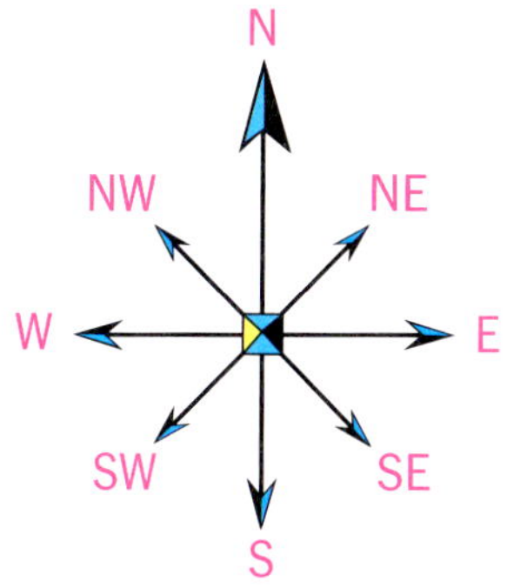

C. Use the compass rose to help with the following directions on the map.

1. Is Hawaii east or west of California?

   west

2. Choose a point on the west coast of the mainland. If you were going from this point to the state of Hawaii, in which direction would you be going?

   southwest

3. If you were going from the "Big Island" Hawaii to the west coast of the mainland, in which direction would you be going?

   northeast

4. If you were going from the "Big Island" Hawaii, to Honolulu, the capital of the state of Hawaii, in which direction would you be going?

   northwest

Activity Objective: Explore Hawaii as a community of natural geographical wonders.
Cross-Curricular Connection: Language Arts — Effectively gathers/uses information for research; asks and seeks to answer questions regarding the characteristics of people and places in one's own community
Almanac: See page 130.

Lesson 18

ACTIVITY

Plan a field trip to the island of Hawaii to study some of its natural wonders.

Exploring Hawaii

The BIG Geographic Question

What are some of Hawaii's unique natural features?

A. Suppose you were taking a field trip to the Big Island in January. You would need to plan transportation from where you live to the Big Island.

1. What form of transportation would you most likely take from where you live? (Most students would probably travel by airplane.)

2. In which direction would you have to travel from your home to Hawaii? (Make sure students' answers reflect where you are located in the U.S.)

B. Using information from the article and Almanac, list on the chart below some places in Hawaii that you would like to visit. Describe each place. One suggestion is shown on the chart for you. (Possible answers may be as follows.)

Places to Visit	Description
Kilauea	the world's most active volcano
Hilo	town where Hawaiians live; farms and plantations
Kailua-Kona	hotels and resorts
Mauna Loa	volcano
Akaka Falls	waterfalls
rain forest	plants and animals

National Geography Standards: 4, 5, 6, 7
Basic Geography Skills: Asking and answering geographic questions
Geographic Themes: Location — Position on Earth's surface; Place — Physical and human characteristics

Informal Assessment: Have students read their postcards aloud. Check to make sure that students accurately describe the natural feature and its location.
Standardized Test-Format Assessment: See page 164.

C. **Now think about the kinds of climate you will find in the places you plan to visit. Use the article and Almanac to find the following information.**

1. What is the average high temperature on Hawaii in January?

   80° Fahrenheit

2. What is the average low temperature on Hawaii in January?

   66° Fahrenheit

3. How does the climate on the east coast of Hawaii differ from the climate on the west coast of Hawaii?

   It's rainier on the east coast.

D. **Think about the clothing you will need to take with you. List and briefly explain why you will need each item.**

(Students' answers should show awareness of differences in climate by planning to bring such items as a swimsuit, a sweater, and a rain jacket.)

E. **Imagine that you are in Hawaii. Using an index card, make a postcard to send home telling what you like about one of Hawaii's natural features. Draw a picture of the natural feature on the front of your card. Write your message on the back.**

(Students' postcards should include details that describe the natural features found on the island.)

ALMANAC

THE SEVEN CONTINENTS
Africa
Antarctica
Asia
Australia
Europe
North America
South America

THE FOUR OCEANS
Arctic
Atlantic
Indian
Pacific

THE FOUR BASIC LANDFORMS
Hills
Mountains
Plains
Plateaus

STATE NAMES	ABBREVIATIONS
Alabama	AL
Alaska	AK
Arizona	AZ
Arkansas	AR
California	CA
Colorado	CO
Connecticut	CT
Delaware	DE
Florida	FL
Georgia	GA
Hawaii	HI
Idaho	ID
Illinois	IL
Indiana	IN
Iowa	IA
Kansas	KS
Kentucky	KY
Louisiana	LA
Maine	ME
Maryland	MD
Massachusetts	MA
Michigan	MI
Minnesota	MN
Mississippi	MS
Missouri	MO
Montana	MT
Nebraska	NE
Nevada	NV
New Hampshire	NH
New Jersey	NJ
New Mexico	NM
New York	NY
North Carolina	NC
North Dakota	ND
Ohio	OH
Oklahoma	OK
Oregon	OR
Pennsylvania	PA
Rhode Island	RI
South Carolina	SC
South Dakota	SD
Tennessee	TN
Texas	TX
Utah	UT
Vermont	VT
Virginia	VA
Washington	WA
West Virginia	WV
Wisconsin	WI
Wyoming	WY

Cape Flattery
Juan de Fuca Strait
Puget Sound
Seattle
Tacoma
Olympia
F.D. Roosevelt Lake
COLUMBIA
PLATEAU
Pend Oreille Lake
Flathead Lake
Mt. Rainier 14,410 ft. (4,392 m.)
RANGE
WASHINGTON
Portland
Columbia River
Mt. Hood 11,235 ft. (3,424 m.)
Salem
CASCADE
COAST RANGES
OREGON
BITTERROOT
ROCKY
RANGE
Helena
Missouri River
Fort Peck Lake
MONTANA
Yellowstone R.
NORTH DAKOTA
Lake Sakakawea
Bismarck
Lake Oahe
SOUTH DAKOTA
Pierre
IDAHO
Borah Peak 12,662 ft. (3,859 m.)
Boise
Grand Teton Peak 13,770 ft. (4,197 m.)
BIGHORN MTNS.
Powder River
BLACK HILLS
GREAT
PLAINS
Missouri
Mt. Shasta 14,162 ft. (4,316 m.)
Goose Lake
Snake River
Continental Divide
WYOMING
Cape Mendocino
River
Sacramento
GREAT BASIN
GREAT SALT LAKE DESERT
Great Salt Lake
RANGE
North Platte River
NEBRASKA
Pyramid Lake
Lake Tahoe
Carson City
Sacramento
Salt Lake City
Utah Lake
MOUNTAINS
Cheyenne
South Platte River
Platte
San Francisco
Oakland
San Jose
SIERRA
NEVADA
Mono Lake
WASATCH
Green River
Republican River
Denver
Mt. Elbert 14,433 ft. (4,399 m.)
KANSAS
San Joaquin R.
Fresno
Pikes Peak 14,110 ft. (4,301 m.)
UTAH
Mt. Whitney 14,494 ft. (4,418 m.)
Death Valley −282 ft. (−89 m.)
Lake Powell
COLORADO
Arkansas
River
Las Vegas
Lake Mead
PAINTED DESERT
COLORADO PLATEAU
SANGRE DE CRISTO MTNS.
CALIFORNIA
Point Conception
MOJAVE DESERT
Grand Canyon
Divide
Santa Fe
Canadian
River
OKLAHOMA
Oklahoma City
PACIFIC OCEAN
Los Angeles
San Bernardino
Riverside
Long Beach
Salton Sea
Colorado
ARIZONA
Rio Grande
NEW MEXICO
Red
River
San Diego
Glendale
Phoenix
Mesa
Gila River
Continental
LLANO ESTACADO
Brazos River
Tucson
TEXAS
Fort Worth
El Paso
GULF OF CALIFORNIA
Colorado River
Pecos River
EDWARDS PLATEAU
Austin
San Antonio
Rio Grande
HAWAII
Kauai Channel
Honolulu
PACIFIC OCEAN
Alenuihaha Channel
Mauna Kea 13,796 ft. (4,205 m.)
100 Miles
100 Kilometers
RUSSIA
Arctic Circle
Pt. Barrow
BROOKS RANGE
ALASKA
Bering Strait
SEWARD PEN.
Yukon River
Tanana River
Mt. McKinley 20,320 ft. (6,194 m.)
ALASKA RANGE
CANADA
BERING SEA
Iliamna Lake
BRISTOL BAY
ALASKA PENINSULA
Shelikof Str.
GULF OF ALASKA
Juneau
ALEUTIAN ISLANDS
250
500 Miles
500 Kilometers
MEXICO
45°
40°
35°
30°
25°
125°
120°
115°
110°
105°
100°
160°
155°
20°
180°
170°
150°
140°
130°
70°
60°
50°

UNITED STATES
National capital
State capital
Major city
International boundary
State boundary
0 150 300 Miles
0 150 300 Kilometers
Projection: Albers Equal Area
CANADA
Lake of the Woods
Red Lake
Lake Superior
MICHIGAN
Lake Huron
Lake Michigan
Lake Ontario
Lake Erie
St. Lawrence River
MAINE
Moosehead Lake
Mt. Washington 6,288 ft. (1,905 m.)
Augusta
Lake Champlain
Montpelier
N.H.
VT.
ADIRONDACK MTNS.
Hudson R.
Concord
Albany
Boston
MASS.
Cape Cod
Syracuse
Rochester
Niagara Falls
Buffalo
NEW YORK
Hartford
Providence
R.I.
New Haven
CONN.
Susquehanna River
Newark
New York
N.J.
Trenton
PENNSYLVANIA
Philadelphia
Harrisburg
Camden
Dover
MD.
Baltimore
Annapolis
Washington
D.C.
DELAWARE BAY
DEL.
ATLANTIC OCEAN
INNESOTA
Minneapolis
St. Paul
Mississippi River
WISCONSIN
Milwaukee
Madison
Grand Rapids
Lansing
Detroit
Chicago
Gary
Hammond
Toledo
Cleveland
Akron
Canton
Youngstown
Pittsburgh
IOWA
Omaha
Des Moines
ILLINOIS
CENTRAL LOWLAND
Springfield
OHIO
Columbus
Dayton
Indianapolis
INDIANA
Cincinnati
Ohio River
WEST VIRGINIA
Charleston
Richmond
Newport News
Norfolk
CHESAPEAKE BAY
VIRGINIA
Roanoke River
Kansas City
peka
Jefferson City
Kansas City
Harry S. Truman Res.
St. Louis
East St. Louis
Wabash R.
Frankfort
Louisville
KENTUCKY
MISSOURI
OZARK PLATEAU
Cumberland River
Knoxville
Nashville
TENNESSEE
APPALACHIAN MOUNTAINS
PLATEAU
Mt. Mitchell 6,684 ft. (2,037 m.)
Winston-Salem
Raleigh
NORTH CAROLINA
Cape Hatteras
Tulsa
ARKANSAS
R.S. Kerr Res.
Memphis
Lake Eufaula
Little Rock
Mississippi River
Tennessee R.
CUMBERLAND
Columbia
SOUTH CAROLINA
Atlanta
Chattahoochee R.
GEORGIA
Birmingham
ALABAMA
Alabama R.
Montgomery
COASTAL PLAIN
ake exoma
Dallas
LOUISIANA
Toledo Bend Res.
Sam Rayburn Reservoir
Jackson
MISSISSIPPI
Jacksonville
Tallahassee
Lake Pontchartrain
Baton Rouge
New Orleans
Houston
FLORIDA
Orlando
Cape Canaveral
Tampa
St. Petersburg
Lake Okeechobee
Miami
Cape Sable
Key West
Straits of Florida
GULF OF MEXICO
N
THE BAHAMAS
CUBA
45°
40°
35°
30°
25°
65°
70°
95°
90°
85°
80°
75°

ARCTIC OCEAN
North Pole
RUSSIA
CHUKCHI SEA
Bering Strait
SEWARD PEN.
Point Barrow
BEAUFORT SEA
ALASKA (U.S.)
Yukon River
Fairbanks
Anchorage
ALASKA RANGE
Mt. McKinley 20,320 ft. (6,194 m.)
Mt. Logan 19,850 ft. (6,050 m.)
GULF OF ALASKA
Juneau
ALEXANDER ARCHIPELAGO
QUEEN CHARLOTTE ISLANDS
VANCOUVER ISLAND
Vancouver
Victoria
Seattle
Portland
PACIFIC OCEAN
CASCADE RANGE
COLUMBIA PLATEAU
Whitehorse
COAST MOUNTAINS
MACKENZIE MOUNTAINS
ROCKY
Mackenzie River
Great Bear Lake
Great Slave Lake
Peace R.
Athabasca R.
Lake Athabasca
Reindeer Lake
Churchill R.
Nelson R.
Churchill
Fraser R.
Columbia R.
Snake
Spokane
Edmonton
Calgary
North Saskatchewan
South
Regina
Lake Manitoba
Lake Winnipeg
Winnipeg
GREAT
CANADA
UNITED STATES
CANADIAN SHIELD
Lake Superior
Lake Huron
Lake Ontario
Ottawa
Montreal
Quebec
Lawrence R.
GULF OF ST. LAWRENCE
Halifax
Cape Sable
LABRADOR
Smallwood Res.
LABRADOR SEA
UNGAVA PEN.
Hudson Strait
HUDSON BAY
BAFFIN ISLAND
BAFFIN BAY
Davis Strait
VICTORIA ISLAND
QUEEN ELIZABETH ISLANDS
ELLESMERE ISLAND
Nares Str.
KALAALLIT NUNAAT (GREENLAND) (DENMARK)
Denmark Strait
Arctic Circle
70°
80°

NORTH AMERICA
National capital
Major city
Other city
International boundary
0 250 500 750 Miles
0 250 500 750 Kilometers
Projection: Azimuthal Equal Area
N
120°
110°
100°
90°
80°
Equator
San Francisco
San Jose
NEVADA
BASIN
Salt Lake
Salt Lake City
Mt. Whitney
14,494 ft.
(4,418 m.)
Death Valley
-282 ft.
(-89 m.)
Colorado
COLORADO PLATEAU
Grand Canyon
Los Angeles
San Diego
Tijuana
Phoenix
Santa Fe
Denver
Platte R.
Arkansas
Omaha
Kansas City
Red R.
El Paso
Fort Worth
Dallas
Ciudad Juárez
Rio Grande
San Antonio
Houston
GUADALUPE I. (MEX.)
BAJA CALIFORNIA PEN.
GULF OF CALIFORNIA
Chihuahua
MEXICO
SIERRA MADRE OCCIDENTAL
Monterrey
MEXICAN PLATEAU
SIERRA MADRE ORIENTAL
Cape San Lucas
Tampico
Guadalajara
León
REVILLAGIGEDO IS. (MEX.)
Mexico City
Puebla
Veracruz
Balsas R.
Acapulco
Citlaltépetl
18,700 ft.
(5,700 m.)
CAMPECHE BAY
GULF OF MEXICO
Cape Catoche
Mérida
YUCATÁN PEN.
BELIZE
GUATEMALA
EL SALVADOR
HONDURAS
San Pedro Sula
NICARAGUA
Lake Nicaragua
COSTA RICA
PANAMA
GULF OF PANAMÁ
CENTRAL AMERICA
Chicago
Des Moines
Indianapolis
Cleveland
Columbus
Cincinnati
Erie
Pittsburgh
Philadelphia
Baltimore
Washington
Norfolk
Cape Hatteras
St. Louis
OZARK PLATEAU
Ohio R.
Mississippi River
Tennessee R.
Memphis
APPALACHIAN
Atlanta
COASTAL PLAIN
New Orleans
Jacksonville
Tampa
Miami
ATLANTIC OCEAN
THE BAHAMAS
Nassau
TURKS AND CAICOS IS. (U.K.)
Straits of Florida
Havana
CUBA
Camagüey
Santiago de Cuba
Yucatán Channel
DOMINICAN REPUBLIC
HAITI
Port-au-Prince
Santo Domingo
JAMAICA
Kingston
CAYMAN IS. (U.K.)
GULF OF HONDURAS
CARIBBEAN SEA
Cape Gracias a Dios
ARUBA (NETH.)
ST. VINCENT AND

THE WORLD PHYSICAL/POLITICAL

- ● World's most populous cities
- —— International boundary
- - - - Disputed boundary
- ······ Undefined boundary

0 — 1000 — 2000 Miles
0 — 1000 — 2000 Kilometers

Projection: Robinson

CENTRAL AMERICA AND WEST INDIES

Projection: Bipolar Oblique Conic Conformal

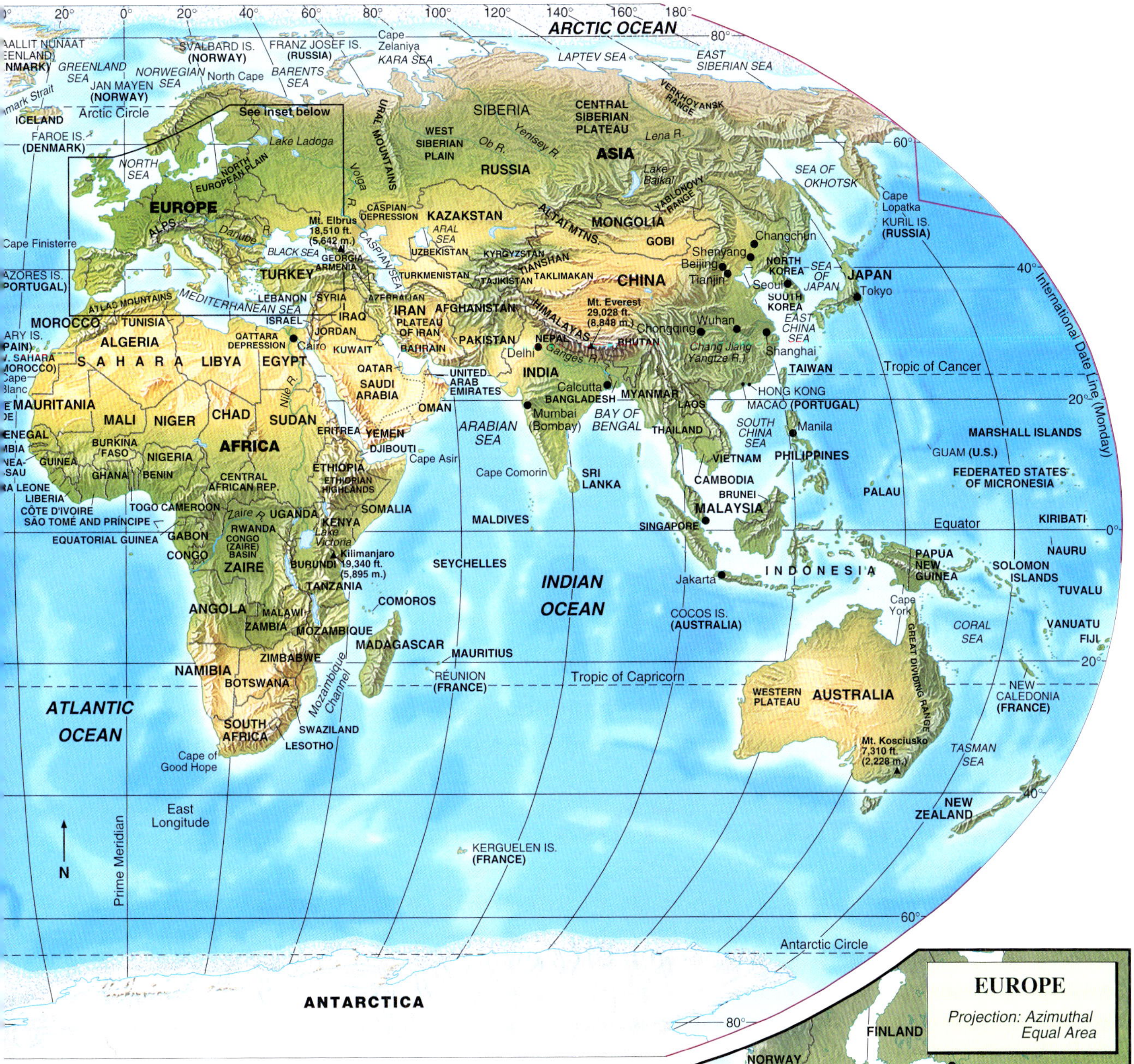
ARCTIC OCEAN
SVALBARD IS. (NORWAY)
FRANZ JOSEF IS. (RUSSIA)
Cape Zelaniya
KARA SEA
LAPTEV SEA
EAST SIBERIAN SEA
GREENLAND SEA
NORWEGIAN SEA
JAN MAYEN (NORWAY)
North Cape
BARENTS SEA
ICELAND
Arctic Circle
FAROE IS. (DENMARK)
See inset below
Lake Ladoga
NORTH SEA
NORTH EUROPEAN PLAIN
EUROPE
ALPS
Danube R.
Volga R.
URAL MOUNTAINS
WEST SIBERIAN PLAIN
SIBERIA
Ob R.
Yenisey R.
CENTRAL SIBERIAN PLATEAU
Lena R.
VERKHOYANSK RANGE
RUSSIA
ASIA
Lake Baikal
YABLONOVYY RANGE
SEA OF OKHOTSK
Cape Lopatka
KURIL IS. (RUSSIA)
CASPIAN DEPRESSION
KAZAKSTAN
ARAL SEA
ALTAI MTNS.
MONGOLIA
GOBI
Mt. Elbrus 18,510 ft. (5,642 m.)
CASPIAN SEA
BLACK SEA
GEORGIA
ARMENIA
AZERBAIJAN
UZBEKISTAN
KYRGYZSTAN
TIANSHAN
TURKMENISTAN
TAJIKISTAN
TAKLIMAKAN
CHINA
Changchun
Shenyang
Beijing
Tianjin
NORTH KOREA
SEA OF JAPAN
Seoul
SOUTH KOREA
JAPAN
Tokyo
Cape Finisterre
AZORES IS. (PORTUGAL)
TURKEY
MEDITERRANEAN SEA
ATLAS MOUNTAINS
LEBANON
SYRIA
ISRAEL
IRAQ
IRAN
PLATEAU OF IRAN
AFGHANISTAN
Mt. Everest 29,028 ft. (8,848 m.)
HIMALAYAS
Chongqing
Wuhan
EAST CHINA SEA
Chang Jiang (Yangtze R.)
Shanghai
TAIWAN
Tropic of Cancer
MOROCCO
TUNISIA
ALGERIA
QATTARA DEPRESSION
Cairo
JORDAN
KUWAIT
BAHRAIN
PAKISTAN
NEPAL
BHUTAN
Delhi
Ganges R.
SAHARA
LIBYA
EGYPT
Nile R.
QATAR
SAUDI ARABIA
UNITED ARAB EMIRATES
INDIA
Calcutta
BANGLADESH
MYANMAR
LAOS
HONG KONG
MACAO (PORTUGAL)
MAURITANIA
MALI
NIGER
CHAD
SUDAN
OMAN
Mumbai (Bombay)
ARABIAN SEA
BAY OF BENGAL
THAILAND
SOUTH CHINA SEA
Manila
MARSHALL ISLANDS
ERITREA
YEMEN
DJIBOUTI
Cape Asir
BURKINA FASO
NIGERIA
AFRICA
GUAM (U.S.)
VIETNAM
PHILIPPINES
GHANA
BENIN
CENTRAL AFRICAN REP.
ETHIOPIA
ETHIOPIAN HIGHLANDS
Cape Comorin
SRI LANKA
CAMBODIA
FEDERATED STATES OF MICRONESIA
LIBERIA
CÔTE D'IVOIRE
TOGO
CAMEROON
SOMALIA
BRUNEI
MALAYSIA
PALAU
SÃO TOMÉ AND PRÍNCIPE
Zaire R.
UGANDA
KENYA
MALDIVES
SINGAPORE
Equator
KIRIBATI
EQUATORIAL GUINEA
GABON
RWANDA
CONGO (ZAIRE) BASIN
Lake Victoria
CONGO
ZAIRE
BURUNDI
Kilimanjaro 19,340 ft. (5,895 m.)
SEYCHELLES
INDIAN OCEAN
Jakarta
INDONESIA
PAPUA NEW GUINEA
NAURU
SOLOMON ISLANDS
TANZANIA
COMOROS
TUVALU
ANGOLA
MALAWI
ZAMBIA
MOZAMBIQUE
COCOS IS. (AUSTRALIA)
Cape York
CORAL SEA
VANUATU
FIJI
MADAGASCAR
MAURITIUS
ZIMBABWE
NAMIBIA
BOTSWANA
Mozambique Channel
RÉUNION (FRANCE)
Tropic of Capricorn
GREAT DIVIDING RANGE
NEW CALEDONIA (FRANCE)
ATLANTIC OCEAN
WESTERN PLATEAU
AUSTRALIA
SOUTH AFRICA
SWAZILAND
LESOTHO
Cape of Good Hope
Mt. Kosciusko 7,310 ft. (2,228 m.)
TASMAN SEA
NEW ZEALAND
East Longitude
N
Prime Meridian
KERGUELEN IS. (FRANCE)
Antarctic Circle
ANTARCTICA
International Date Line (Monday)

EUROPE
Projection: Azimuthal Equal Area
FINLAND
NORWAY
SWEDEN
St. Petersburg
ESTONIA
Moscow
IRELAND
UNITED KINGDOM
DENMARK
LATVIA
LITHUANIA
RUSSIA
London
NETHERLANDS
BELARUS
N
GERMANY
BELGIUM
POLAND
ATLANTIC OCEAN
LUXEMBOURG
Paris
CZECH REPUBLIC
UKRAINE
FRANCE
SLOVAKIA
SWITZERLAND
AUSTRIA
HUNGARY
MOLDOVA
SLOVENIA
CROATIA
ROMANIA
BOSNIA HERZEGOVINA
SERBIA
PORTUGAL
SPAIN
YUGOSLAVIA
BLACK SEA
GEORGIA
ITALY
BULGARIA
MONTENEGRO
ALBANIA
MACEDONIA
GIBRALTAR (U.K.)
MEDITERRANEAN SEA
GREECE
TURKEY
0 250 500 Miles
0 250 500 Kilometers
TUNISIA
MALTA
CYPRUS
SYRIA
LEBANON

Time Line of Native American and European Settlements in North America

- **1000** Adena in the Midwest
- **1250** Anasazi, or Pueblo, in the Southwest
- **1300** Chinook in the Northwest
- **1500**
  - Iroquois in the Northeast
  - Sioux in the Great Plains
  - Cherokee in the Southeast
- **1565** Spanish in St. Augustine, Florida
- **1607** English in Jamestown, Virginia
- **1609** Spanish in Santa Fe, New Mexico
- **1620** Pilgrims in Plymouth, Massachusetts
- **1630** Puritans in Boston, Massachusetts
- **1635** Dutch in New York City, New York

Source: *The World Book Encyclopedia*, 1991

Regional Native American Tribes

Great Plains Native Americans	Iowa, Kansa, Missouri, Wichita, Comanche, Omaha, Crow, Cheyenne, Sioux, Lakota

Spotlight on: Cheyenne Tribe	
Region	North American Plains near the Platte and Arkansas rivers; in the Black Hills of South Dakota; tall grasslands and rivers
Climate	warm, dry summers; cold winters with blowing snow
Shelter	tepees were made of long poles and buffalo skins which could be easily taken apart and moved
Resources	buffalo used for fuel, food, and clothing; fertile river valley allowed for some farming

Northeast Native Americans (Eastern Woodlands)	Mohawk, Cayuga, Seneca, Oneida, Onondaga, Iroquois, Delaware
Spotlight on: Seneca Tribe	
Region	western New York and eastern Ohio
Climate	warm summers; cold, snowy winters
Shelter	longhouses built of wood and bark
Resources	fertile soil and an abundance of fresh water from the Great Lakes allowed them to cultivate corn and other vegetables; hunted a variety of wild game

Northwest Native Americans	Makah, Haida, Okanagoh, Quinault, Nootka, Chinook, Spokane, Kalapuya, Kalispel, Shuswap
Spotlight on: Makah Tribe	
Region	Northwest Pacific coast of North America; Vancouver Island at northwest tip of Washington state
Climate	mild temperatures due to Pacific Ocean air currents which bring heavy rainfall
Shelter	wooden plank houses
Resources	forests for shelter; salmon, whale, and caribou used for food

Southeast Native Americans	Cherokee, Chickasaw, Choctaw, Creek, Seminole, Powhatan, Natchez, Timicua, Sauk, Caddo
Spotlight on: Cherokee Tribe	
Region	southern Appalachian region; North Carolina and Tennessee
Climate	mild seasons; warm summers and wet winters
Shelter	wigwams: huts with arched frameworks of poles covered with bark or animal hides
Resources	rich soil for farming crops of corn, beans, and squash, along with hunting wild game such as deer and birds

Southwest Native Americans	Navajo, Apache, Hopi, Pima, Pueblo, Papago, Cochimi
Spotlight on: Pueblo Tribe	
Region	Four Corners—where Utah, Colorado, Arizona, and New Mexico meet; desert terrain with many cliffs, canyons, and rock formations
Climate	hot and dry with little rain
Shelter	houses built of adobe in cliffs; large apartment-like dwellings for many families with 20 to 1000 rooms
Resources	desert soil good for growing crops such as beans, cotton, and corn; also used to make clay for pottery

Sources: *The World Book Encyclopedia*, 1991 and *Man in Nature*, Carl Sauer, 1980

Historical Native American Shelters

Panoan house

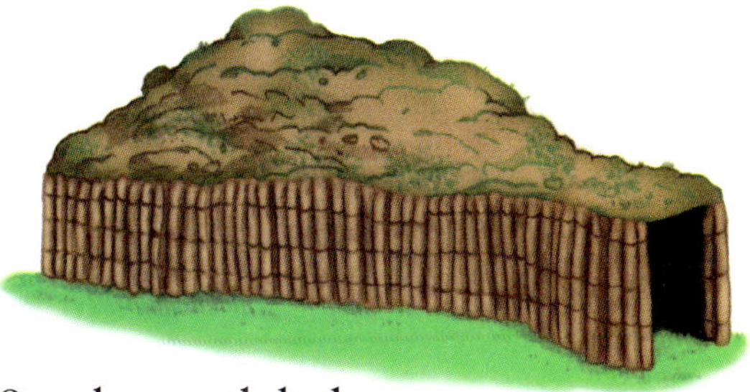
Omaha earth lodge

Interior Salish earth house

Navajo hogan

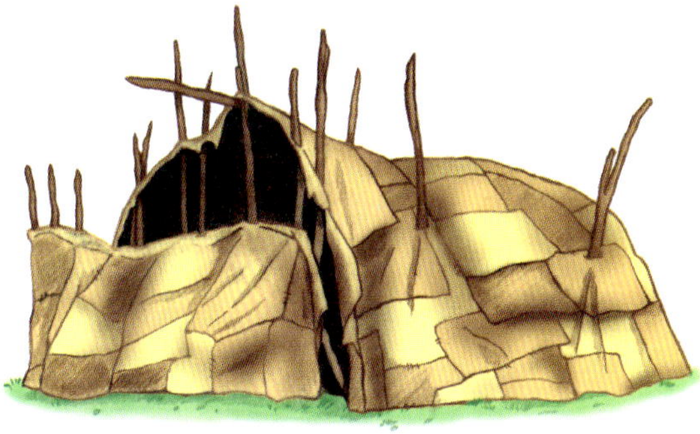
Tehuelche hut

Inca masonry and thatch hut

Arawak thatch hut

A Look at Jamestown Through Time

1607

- Jamestown was settled.
- The ground was swampy and the water impure.
- A meager diet weakened the settlers and over half of them soon died of dysentery, malnutrition, malaria, and pneumonia.

1609

- Captain John Smith returned to England for treatment of an injury caused by an accident.
- The settlers had a terrible winter and suffered from hunger.

1611

- The settlers gave up trying to produce silk and grapes.
- They began raising hogs and corn.
- Shipbuilding, glass-blowing, and iron smelting soon began.

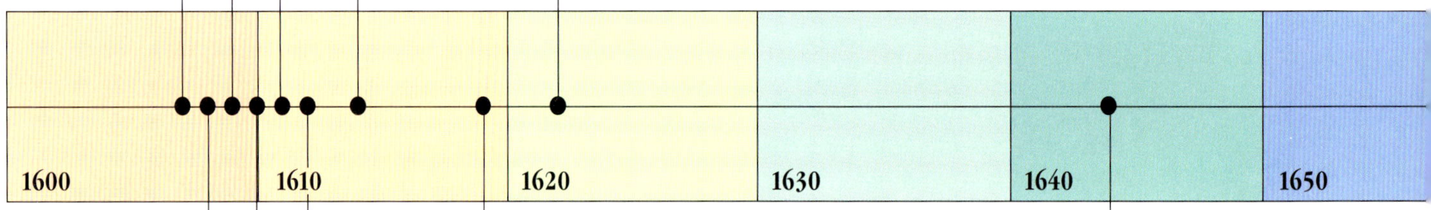

1608

- Captain John Smith took control of the settlement.
- He taught the settlers to follow the Native Americans' farming example and urged them to stop looking for gold.

1610

- Governor Thomas West, Lord De La Warr, arrived with supplies and more settlers.

1612

- John Rolfe brought a new type of tobacco from Trinidad. It was a good crop for Jamestown to sell in England.

1614

- John Rolfe married Pocahontas which brought five years of peace between the settlers and the Native Americans.

1622

- The Native Americans and settlers began to fight.

1699

- Fire destroyed the settlement again.
- Jamestown was ruined.
- The settlers changed their capital to Williamsburg.

1957

- Virginia rebuilt Jamestown to look like the early settlement.

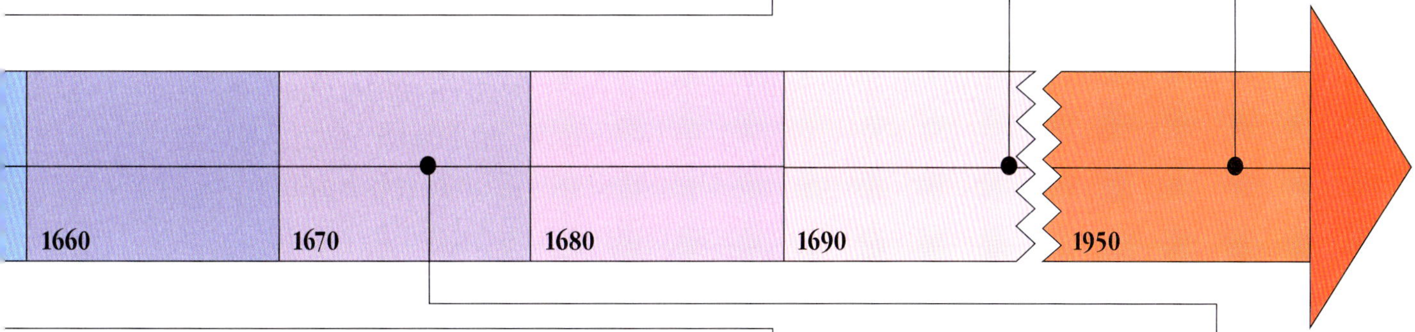

1619

- A lawmaking assembly called the House of Burgesses was started.
- A Dutch ship brought Africans who were sold as slaves to the colony. Slave labor was used to help the colony prosper.

1644

- The Native Americans and settlers fought again.

1676

- Fire destroyed Jamestown during Bacon's Rebellion. Planter Nathaniel Bacon led the revolt against the royal governor William Berkely.

Source: *The World Book Encyclopedia*, 1991

Further Fort Facts

The Alamo • San Antonio, TX

Established as a Catholic mission by the Spanish in 1744, the Alamo consisted of a church and living quarters. It was surrounded by high walls which guarded against enemy attacks. The mission was called the Alamo, the Spanish name for the cottonwood trees surrounding it. It was built of adobe. Adobe is large blocks of mud baked hard in the sun. The Alamo became famous during the Mexican-American War (1846–1848).

Fort Ticonderoga • Fort Ticonderoga, NY

Established by the French in 1755, several different flags have flown over Fort Ticonderoga. It has been controlled by France, and twice each by Britain and the United States. The fort is built in a star shape. It was built to control an invasion route to Canada. Fort Ticonderoga became a stronghold during the Revolutionary War (1775–1781).

Fort Mackinac • Mackinac Island, MI

On a wooded island in Lake Huron high on a bluff, the British built this fort in 1780. A large ramp and fortress were built of limestone, which was plentiful in the area during that time. Fort Mackinac was surrounded by tall timber fences. Many log living quarters were built within the wooden walls.

Isolated Communities of the Past

Buffalo, New York 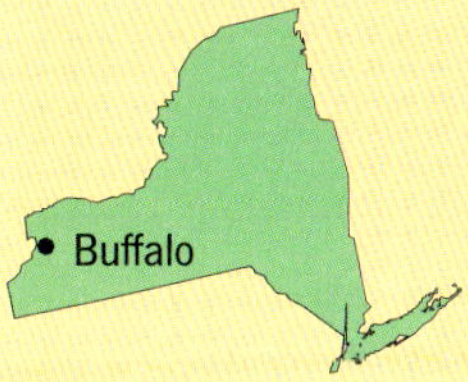	1803	• The Holland Land Company settled at the head of the Niagara River. The community was called New Amsterdam, but settlers called it Buffalo from Buffalo Creek, a nearby stream.
	1825	• The Erie Canal was built to provide an all-water route to New York City. The canal enabled Buffalo to become an important trade center linking the east and the west.
	1840	• The world's first grain elevator was built in Buffalo. It processed grain shipped from the west over the Great Lakes, then transported the grain to the east on the Erie canal.
	1896	• Large-scale production of electricity began at Niagara Falls.

Salt Lake City, Utah 	1847	• The city was founded by 148 Mormon pioneers, led by Brigham Young. Utah was not under United States law. This was important to the Mormons because they did not agree with the United States' rules. • Named for the Great Salt Lake, Salt Lake City is in a valley, surrounded by mountains.
	1850	• Almost 5,000 Mormons lived in the city by this time. • Utah became a United States Territory, and Brigham Young became its first governor.
	1863	• Lead and silver were discovered in Brigham Canyon.
	1869	• Workers laid the tracks that completed the nation's first transcontinental railroad. Salt Lake City could now easily transport its farm and mining products out of the area.
	1896	• Utah became a state, with Salt Lake City as its capital.

Types of Communities

City (or Urban area)	an area with 2,500 or more people, usually including a centralized city and nearby smaller communities
Community	a place where people live, work, and have fun together
Edge city	suburban downtown areas that include shopping malls, office complexes, and industrial parks that are developed near major expressways
Metropolitan area	a large city and its inner and outer suburbs
Rural area	farms and towns in uncrowded areas with fewer than 2,500 people
Suburb	a community near or on the outskirts of a city. Almost half of all Americans live in suburbs.
Town	a cluster of houses and other buildings in which people work and live. Usually it is smaller than a city, but larger than a village.
Village	any small group of houses and dwellings. A village is often a trade and social center of a township and has a president and a board of trustees.

Source: *The World Book Encyclopedia*, 1991

Kinds of Roads	Abbreviations
Avenue	Ave.
Boulevard	Blvd.
Court	Ct.
Drive	Dr.
Freeway	Fwy.
Highway	Hwy.
Interstate	I
Lane	Ln.
Parkway	Pkwy.
Point	Pt.
Road	Rd.
Square	Sq.
Street	St.

Community Resources

- Library*
- Fire Station
- Post Office
- Police Station
- City Hall
- Chamber of Commerce*
- Grocery Store
- Gas Station
- Hardware Store
- Bank
- Pharmacy
- Video Store
- School
- Church
- College
- Park
- Sports Arena
- Courthouse*
- Barber/Beauty Shop
- Auto Repair Shop
- Shopping Mall
- Hospital
- Restaurant
- Pool

* Resource you can visit or write to for more information about your community

A Mental Map of Place in Space

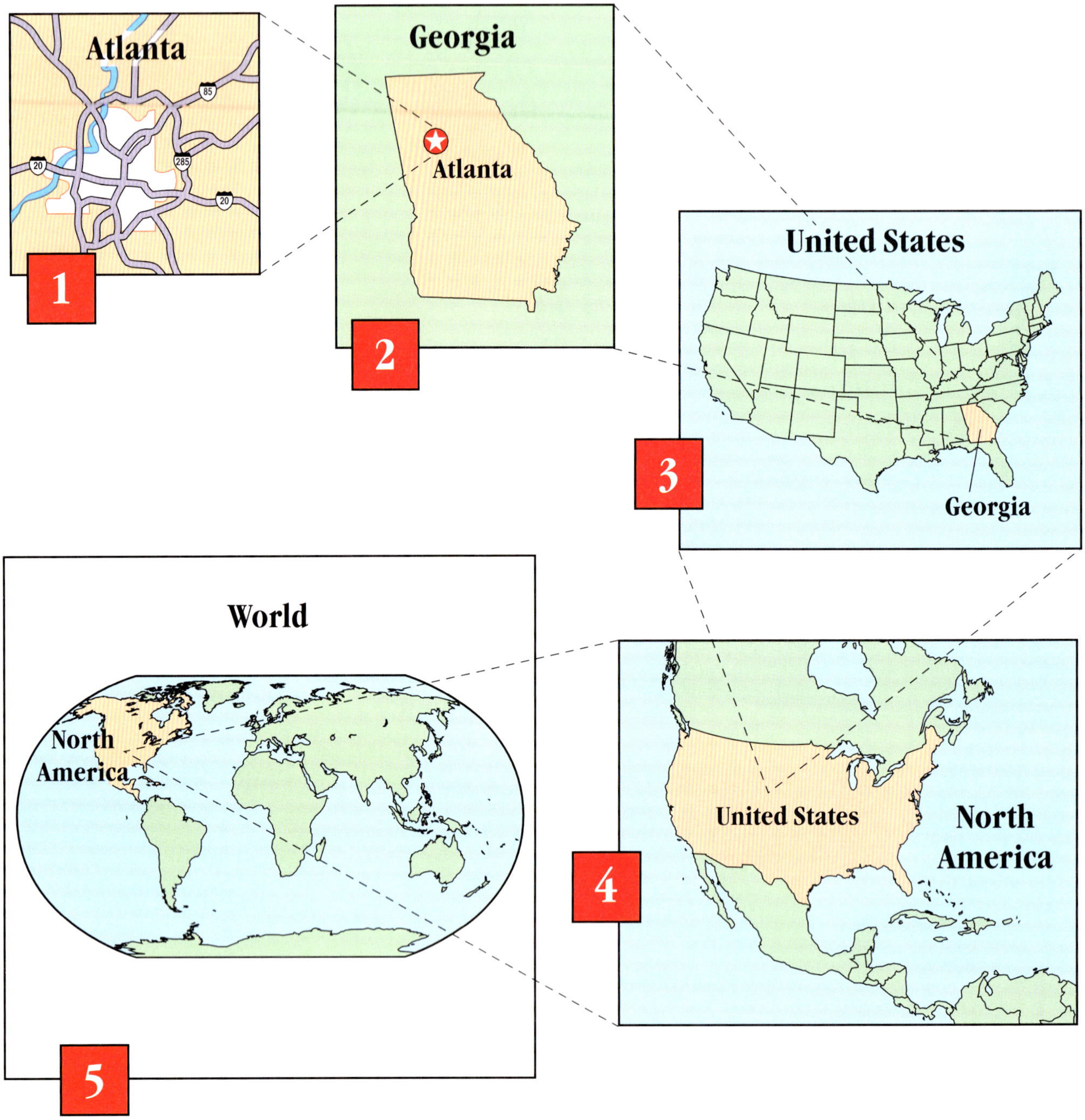

Population Density of the United States, 1995

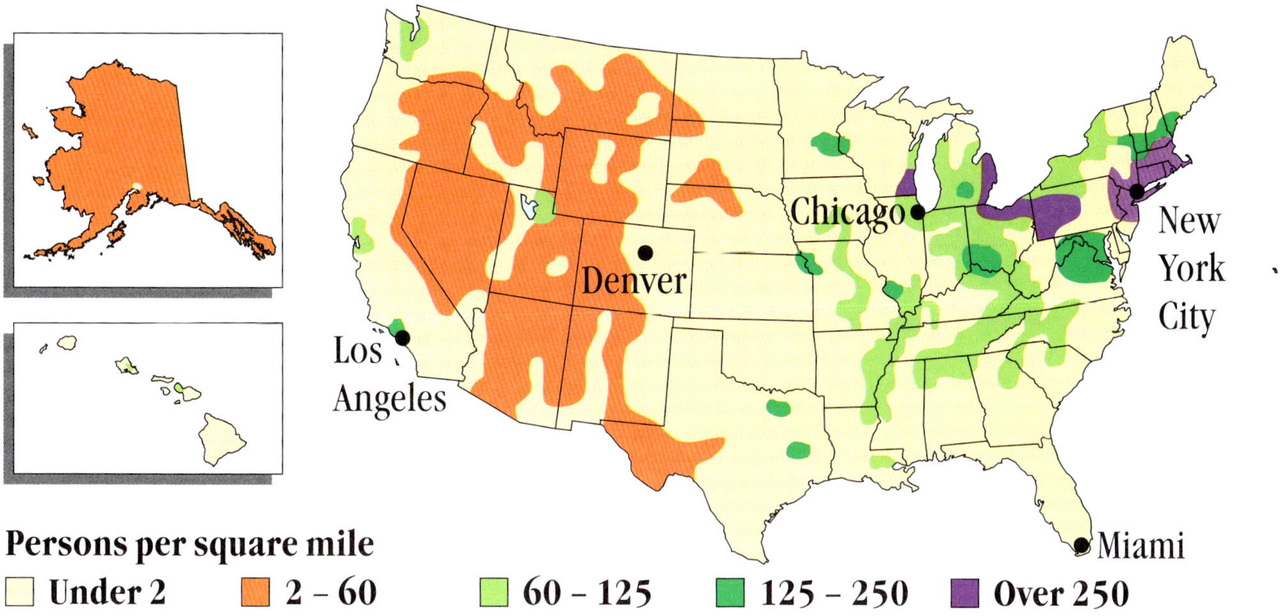

Community Recreational Activities

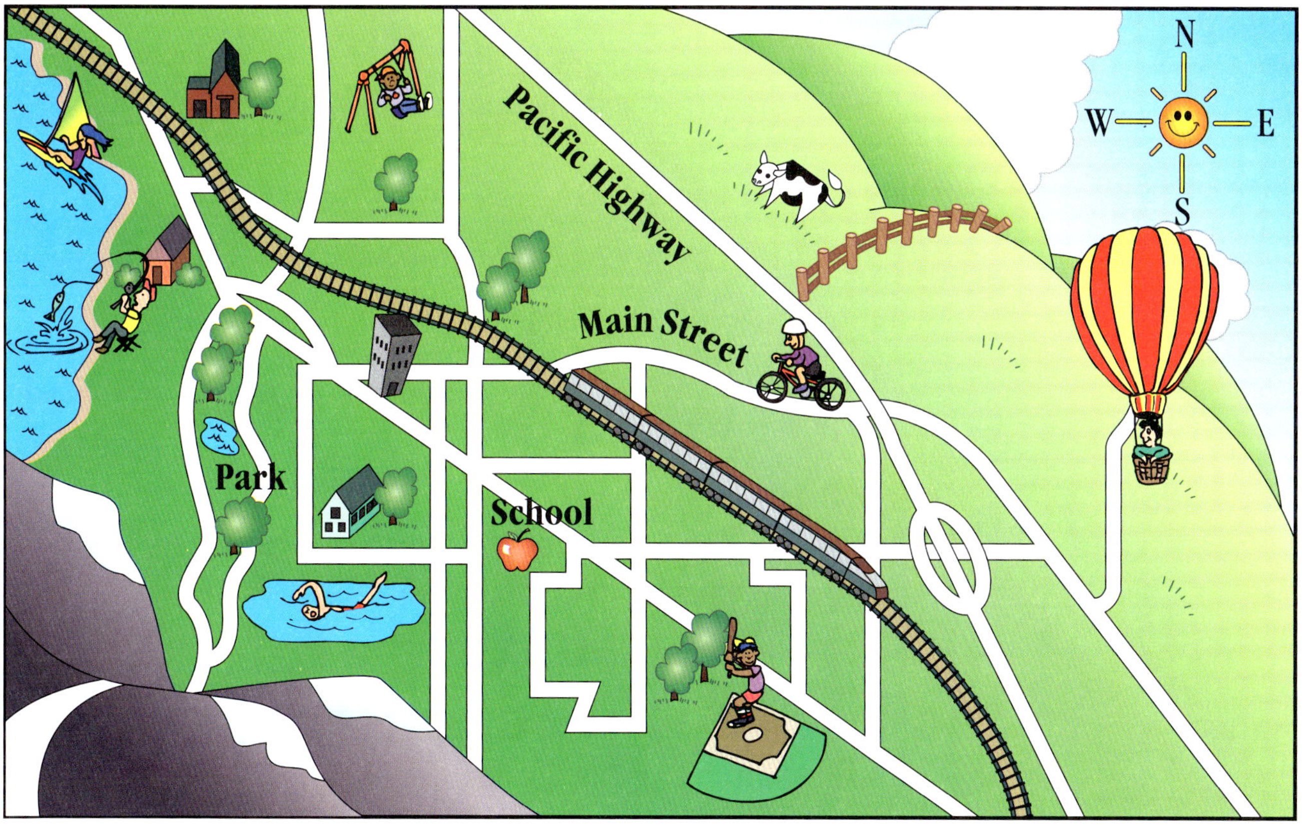

Interesting Facts About Hawaii

- Largest industry: tourism
- Major products: pineapples, sugarcane, fish, printing and publishing, macadamia nuts
- Mauna Loa in Hawaii Volcanoes National Park is the largest active volcano in the United States. It erupts about once every three and a half years.
- Mt. Waialeale, on the island of Kauai, is the rainiest place in the world. Its average rainfall is about 460 inches a year.

Source: *The World Book Encyclopedia*, 1991; *The 1996 World Almanac and Book of Facts*, Funk & Wagnalls

Average Temperature

	Highs	Lows
January	80	66
July	88	74

Population of Three Largest Cities in Hawaii

Rank	City	Population
1	Honolulu (capital city)	377,059
2	Hilo	37,808
3	Kailua Kona	36,818

More About Houston

Founded	1836
Population	1,629,902 (the 4th largest city in the United States)
Average Temperature	January – 55°F July – 83°F
Transportation	An intercontinental and a smaller airport; passenger trains and freight rail lines; an underground tunnel system; major freeways
Recreation	Over 400 parks, Houston Zoo, Houston Symphony, Houston Oilers football team, Houston Astros baseball team, Houston Rockets basketball team, and Houston Livestock Show and Rodeo
Industry	Shipping, oil refining, National Aeronautics and Space Administration (NASA), medical research, textiles, paper products, and machinery production

Source: *The World Book Encyclopedia*, 1991

More About The Four Fabulous Communities

City	Geography	Products	First Settlements and Changes Over Time
Phoenix, Arizona	• Lies in the Salt River Valley, a flat region surrounded by low mountains • Warm, sunny, dry climate	• Railroads made Phoenix a center for trading and processing farm products • Aircraft manufacturing	• Hohokam Native American tribe • United States military post in 1865 • Irrigation canals were used to bring water from the Salt and Gila rivers.
St. Paul, Minnesota	• Located on the banks of the Mississippi River • Dry, cool climate • Fertile land for growing wheat	• Important transportation center due to railroads, airports, and the Mississippi River • Automobiles, transportation equipment, cosmetics, and machinery	• Sioux Native American tribe • Founded in 1840 as an important fur-trading post and a busy river port
Oklahoma City, Oklahoma	• Located near the North Canadian River • Warm, dry climate	• Building materials, cottonseed oil, iron and steel products, paper products • Nation's leading cattle market	• Creek and Seminole Native American tribes • Federal government bought the land in 1889 • Several water reservoirs had to be built
Richmond, Virginia	• Located near the James River • Wet, warm climate • Fertile land for tobacco farming	• Tobacco products, machinery for manufacturing tobacco products, food products, and paper	• Powhatan Native American tribe • Fort Charles built in 1644 to attract settlers • Settlers set up trading posts for furs, hides, and tobacco

Source: *1996 Information Please Almanac,* Otto Johnson, editor

Spotlight on Urban Communities

San Francisco, CA	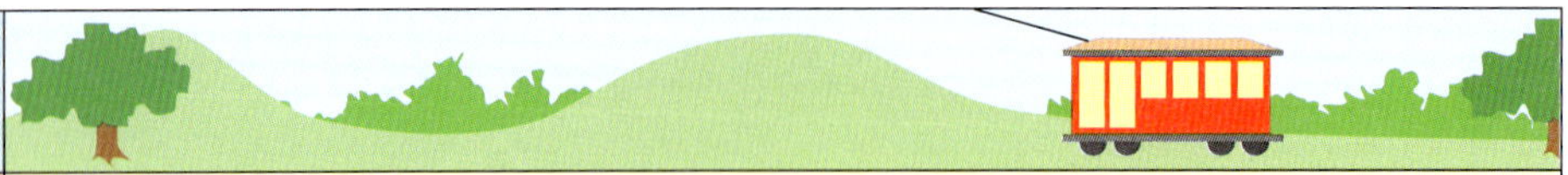
Cultural Activities	• War Memorial Opera House • Louise M. Davies Symphony • Herbst Theater (music, dance, and theater performances) • Asian Art Museum • San Francisco Museum of Modern Art • Morrison Planetarium • Steinhart Aquarium
Professional Sports	• San Francisco 49ers–football • San Francisco Giants–baseball
Industry	• Garment making • Food processing • Producing electronic equipment • Printing and publishing • Banking • Tourism • Ports
Transportation	• San Francisco International Airport • Electronic rail system–Bay Area Rapid Transit (BART) • Cable cars, buses, trolleys
Recreational Activities	• Boating and sailing • 160 parks and playgrounds • San Francisco Zoo • Muir National Forest (giant redwood forest)

Chicago, IL	
Cultural Activities	• Chicago Symphony Orchestra • Goodman Theater* • Steppenwolf Theater* • Court in Hyde Park* • Field Museum of Natural History • John G. Shedd Aquarium • Adler Planetarium • The Art Institute of Chicago • DuSable Museum of African American History (*Broadway shows, classics, and comedies)
Professional Sports	• Chicago Bears–football • Chicago Cubs and Chicago White Sox–baseball • Chicago Bulls–basketball
Industry	• Service industry • Clothing • Industrial and atomic research • Ports • Chicago Stock Exchange • Publishing
Transportation	• 3 Airports–O'Hare International (world's busiest airport), Chicago Midway Airport, Meigs Field • Chicago Transit Authority (CTA)–Bus lines, elevated subway, ground level trains
Recreational Activities	• 560 parks and playgrounds • Cook County Forest Preserves

Source: *The World Book Encyclopedia,* 1991

Glossary

A

adapt: to learn to do something

adobe: a sandy clay mixed with straw used for making bricks

artifacts: old items that tell us about a group of people

artificial: not natural, usually human-made

B

bayou: a creek or minor river

box canyon: a valley so steep its walls seem almost vertical

business: the occupation, work, or trade in which a person is engaged

C

cardinal directions: north, south, east, and west

cartographer: someone who draws maps

commute: to travel daily by car, bus, or train to work

compass rose: a map symbol that shows directions

continent: a large body of land made up of many countries

coquina: a soft limestone commonly found in Florida

cultural activities: activities related to art or learning

D

desert: a large, dry area of land with little or no rainfall

dredging: cleaning, deepening, and widening a waterway

E

environment: surroundings and features of a place

equator: an imaginary line around Earth's surface halfway between the North and South poles

G

geographer: a person who studies Earth's surface

globe: a model of Earth on which shapes, areas, distances, and directions are all shown

grid: a system of lines that form boxes

gulf: an area of ocean or sea partially surrounded by curved land

H

hill: a high landform, not as tall as a mountain

historical map: a map that gives information about the past

I

indigo: a plant from which purple dye is made

intermediate directions: northwest, southwest, northeast, southeast

island: a piece of land surrounded by water on all sides

isolated: cut off from or not connected to other people or places

L

lake: a large body of water surrounded by land

lava: melted rock that flows out of volcanoes

legend: a map key that explains the symbols on a map

locator map: a map that helps find where a certain place is

M

mainland: the one big piece of land that makes up the United States

manufacturing: making or producing a product, especially large-scale and by machines

map scale: a feature used to figure out distance from one place to another on a map

map title: the label that tells what a map is about

map: a drawing of all or part of Earth's surface on a flat piece of paper

mental map: a way of organizing information in your mind

metropolitan area: a large city and its inner and outer suburbs

mountain: peaked land that rises very high above the land around it

N

natural: made by nature

O

ocean: the biggest body of water that surrounds land

P

peninsula: an area of land surrounded by water on three sides

physical map: a map that shows different landforms and water forms

plain: a broad area of low, level land

plateau: a large area of high, flat land

population: all of the people living in a certain area

prairie: land that has many different kinds of grasses growing on it

prime meridian: the starting point to measure both east and west around the globe; located in Greenwich, England

R

rain shadow: a process in which cool winds from the ocean produce rain that falls in the mountains

resource: something natural or human-made, that people use

river: a large stream of water that flows through land

S

suburb: a place where people live that is close to or on the outer edge of a city

T

trade: the business of buying and selling goods

transportation: a system for moving passengers and goods from one place to another

INDEX

A

B

C

D

E

F

G

PROFESSIONAL HANDBOOK

TABLE OF CONTENTS

PROGRAM PHILOSOPHY
STRENGTHENING GEOGRAPHY

So what exactly is geography? It is an integrative discipline that brings together the physical and human dimensions of the world in the study of people, places, and environments. Its subject matter is Earth's surface and the processes that shape it, the relationships between people and environments, and the connections between people and places.
– *Geography for Life, National Geography Standards 1994*

In 1994 thirty percent of fourth graders in the United States scored below the basic level on the National Assessment of Educational Progress in Geography. Only three percent scored at or above advanced level. NAEP tested students not just on their knowledge of locations and map skills, but on applying that knowledge in three content areas:

- **Space and Place:**
  Knowledge of geography related to particular places on Earth, to spatial patterns on Earth's surface, and to physical and human processes that shape such patterns.
- **Environment and Society:**
  Knowledge of geography related to the interactions between environment and society.
- **Spatial Dynamics and Connections:**
  Knowledge of geography as it relates to spatial connections among people, places, and regions.

SRA Geography was developed in response to public concern about students' lack of geographic skills and understanding. Within a full elementary curriculum of reading, language arts, math, science, art, health, and music and within the context of elementary social studies, geography is often neglected. *SRA Geography* is uniquely designed to perfectly align with most state guidelines for social studies at grades 3–6 so that it can easily be used to strengthen the geography strand of *any* elementary social studies program.

SRA Geography was developed in response to public concern about students' lack of geographic skills and understanding.

Map skills are fundamental to understanding geography. But geography involves much more than the ability to read different kinds of maps and to memorize place names. That's why *SRA Geography* incorporates a comprehensive introduction to varieties of map skills within the context of the geographic concepts and social studies subject matter. Students learn to read maps and at the same time they apply that knowledge to further their understanding of relationships among people, places, and environments. Each of the 18 lessons at each grade level of the program includes a map skill lesson that relates to and expands understanding of the lesson's geography concept.

Geographers are also researchers. They ask: Where is something? Why is it there? How did it get there? How does it interact with other things? *SRA Geography* was developed to teach students to ask these questions themselves and to show them how to find the answers. Each lesson includes an activity that leads students through the process of asking questions, gathering information, drawing conclusions, and summarizing their findings. The lesson article and the Almanac in the back of each student book provide facts and details to facilitate the development of research and critical thinking skills.

Earth is becoming more crowded, the environment is threatened, and communications and the economy are global. Studying geography and learning to ask and research geographic questions at an early age will help to make our young citizens better able to understand global issues and make informed decisions about them. *SRA Geography* provides a simple way to strengthen geographic understanding.

What is Geography?

by Cathy L. Salter

For too long, the study of geography was thought to be little more than the memorization of state capitals and exercises in map location. But geography is much more than that. Geography is the science of space and place on Earth's surface. An essential aspect of geography is a knowledge of the physical and human characteristics of all Earth's features. Beyond that, the subject matter of geography is closely related to many other disciplines that students will study–economics, sociology, anthropology, history, and earth science.

Geography investigates *where* something is, *why* it is there, and *how* it got there.

Geography investigates *where* something is, *why* it is there, and *how* it got there. Students need to think about why a place is located where it is, what it is like, the significance of its location, and the issues that affect it. Geography analyzes how people and places are arranged spatially over Earth's surface. It helps us appreciate the relationships among people, places, and environments. The power and beauty of geography is in seeing and understanding the complex world in which we live.

Geographic Questions

The drought of 1996, which affected areas of Texas and parts of the Lower Plains and American Southwest, highlights concerns related to geography. Just locating where the drought occurred does not address all of the geographic aspects of the issue. To understand the depth and significance of the drought, today's students need to ask *geographic* questions.

For example:

- Where is the region affected by the drought?
- How is the land currently being used?
- Will the effects of the drought be felt beyond the region?
- What special demands has the drought made on the available water supply of the region's urban centers?
- Should farmers not plant crops that require extensive irrigation in this region?
- How can wheat and cattle farmers in the region survive an extended drought?
- What will other long-range effects of the drought be on the people and economy of the region?
- Are there lessons from the past that will prepare people to deal with these types of environmental concerns?

The subject of geography encompasses all these questions and more.

Geographic Skills

Knowing and understanding are important elements of geography, but they alone will not prepare students to deal with real-world issues. Equally important are the geographic skills of critical thinking, problem solving, and inquiry. Geographic skills are building blocks essential to the development of a geographic perspective. They include asking and answering geographic questions, analyzing and solving problems, evaluating the consequences of different courses of action, and accepting the fact that there are diverse ways of looking at and interacting with the environment.

continued

Real-World Issues

Developing an understanding of geographic issues, asking geographic questions, and using geographic skills prepare students to become informed decision makers and citizens of the world inside and outside school. In five years Fresh Kills landfill on New York's Staten Island will be closed. New York City is faced with the problem of exporting 400 truckloads of trash collected daily to landfill sites around the east coast. As population pressures continue to make demands on land resources, local issues easily become regional and even global concerns. Geographic literacy enables students to make better sense of the world and become responsible and informed participants in important issues that affect them and those around them. A knowledge of geography helps students understand how people depend upon, adapt to, are affected by, and change the natural environment. In a rapidly expanding and increasingly interconnected world, geography can also help students become familiar with foreign markets and world resources, cultures, and languages.

***SRA Geography* supports the belief that a knowledge and understanding of geography will enable students to understand the diversity of the people who share Earth's finite resources and to become more effective stewards of their place on the planet.**

Why Study Geography?

Geography instruction alone will not manage the world's environment and resources or settle international trade disputes. But it is essential that today's students understand the connections among places and recognize that local actions can have global effects. In the coming century Earth will become more crowded, the physical environment of the globe will be more threatened, finite natural resources will be even more in demand, technological advances will make world events more interconnected, and the global economy will become even more competitive. *SRA Geography* supports the belief that a knowledge and understanding of geography will enable students to understand the diversity of the people who share Earth's finite resources and to become more effective stewards of their place on the planet.

Bringing Geography up to Standards: A History

by James F. Marran

At long last, in *Geography for Life: National Geography Standards* (1994), American schools have a set of National Standards designed to provide geographically appropriate guiding principles for K–12 curriculum. With the Standards in place, the challenge now is to implement them in lessons and activities that are both teacher-friendly and interesting for students. *SRA Geography* is a response to that challenge. In a set of tightly woven Standards-based lessons, it translates the content of *Geography for Life* into sets of self-contained activities that teachers can use to deepen the quality of geography content in their grades 3–6 social studies program.

SRA Geography recognizes that geography is both simple and complex. It is simple because its basic purpose is to provide students with knowledge and skills necessary to better comprehend the world in which they will live as adults. It is complex because of the array of topics it addresses, the societal issues it joins, and the problems it challenges students to solve. Geography encourages students to look at Earth as a physical object, rich in its fragile ecological diversity, and also as a cultural expression examining how societies situate and organize themselves as well as how individuals within them make their livings, raise their children, and pursue their hopes and dreams. With *SRA Geography*, students learn to look at the whole world through its parts, to understand the connections between those parts, and to recognize how the local affects the global and vice versa.

For too long, the value of geography as a school subject was lost. Somehow its identity was compromised so that it became little more than place identification. The only important geographic question in most classrooms had become: Where *is* it? There was little or no interest in any kind of locational analysis or spatial investigation, in asking the *reason* for its location, how it *relates* to other places, or how it *influences* the lives of those who live there. The power of geography in most schools was reduced to little more than target practice on a map.

Within the last decade or so, however, three significant events have changed the perception of geography as merely an exercise in place location. With the publication of *Guidelines for Geographic Education: Elementary and Secondary* (1984), teachers were introduced to the five fundamental themes (Location, Place, Human /Environmental Interaction, Movement, and Regions) as the content organizers for developing and presenting geography as either a separate subject or as an integrative experience within the social sciences. The themes quickly won wide acceptance. They were clear, concise, and engagingly simple. In a subtle way, they revealed geography's many faces by providing a framework for teaching geography in compelling ways across the grade levels.

Geography encourages students to look at Earth as a physical object, rich in its fragile ecological diversity, and also as a cultural expression examining how societies situate and organize themselves as well as how individuals within them make their livings, raise their children, and pursue their hopes and dreams.

continued

Thus, the themes were catalytic. Their acceptance within the educational community was so positive that the face of school geography changed completely in a relatively short period of time. The five themes were the single most influential factor in geography's success as the K–12 curriculum's renaissance discipline in the late twentieth century.

The reality was validated when geography was identified as a core subject by the nation's governors at their first-ever education summit, which convened at Charlottesville, Virginia, in October 1989. In an unprecedented expression of support, they identified proficiency in geography as one of the national goals for American education by the year 2000. That recognition escalated the discipline to a desperately-needed position of prominence in the curriculum. It also ensured that geography would play a major role in the movement to reform the initiatives for school change mounted by the Bush and Clinton administrations in the 1990s.

With geography now fixed in the firmament of school subjects as a result of the decisions at the National Governor's Conference, the next step was to establish a set of internationally competitive standards identifying what every student in United States schools should understand and know about geography. In response to that need, and building on the enormous success of the five themes, geography educators developed *Geography for Life: National Geography Standards* (1994). The 18 standards presented in the document provide the subject matter, skills, and perspectives of geography organized under six essential elements. These six shaping concepts (the World in Spatial Terms, Places and Regions, Physical Systems, Human Systems, Environment and Society, and the Uses of Geography) define the structure of geography content while complementing and reinforcing the organizing role of the five themes.

Through *SRA Geography,* students see events in the context of spaces and places, and thus are able to appreciate the cause-and-effect relationships and the full breadth of chronological development that made those places an important part of the human experience.

The primary purpose of the National Standards is to provide teachers with a resource for deciding which geographic principles to include, either in freestanding courses or integrated with other subjects in the curriculum. The Standards establish what students should know and be able to do at the end of the benchmark grades (4, 8, and 12) in ways that will ensure competence in geography, and at the same time promote an informed world view.

SRA Geography illustrates how the National Geography Standards can be used to enhance the content of elementary and middle school social studies. The program uses case studies and complementary map activities to engage students in a series of problem-solving exercises from a spatial and ecological perspective. In the spirit of *Geography for Life, SRA Geography* presents geography as both integrative and practical. Each lesson gives attention to the relationship between geography and history by showing the essential nature of place as well as the interaction between people and the physical environment. Through *SRA Geography,* students see events in the context of spaces and places, and thus are able to appreciate the cause-and-effect relationships and the full breadth of chronological development that made those places an important part of the human experience.

Since the mid-1980s the increased role of geography in the schools affirms that its consistent inclusion in the curriculum is essential. *SRA Geography* reminds teachers that the infusion of geography will provide students with insights about the role of geographic concepts as forces in history and also give them a fuller sense of their responsibility toward the environment and other societal issues.

Name ______________________ Date __________

Lesson 1 PAGES 2–7

1. What does the following pie graph show about Earth's four oceans?

____

____

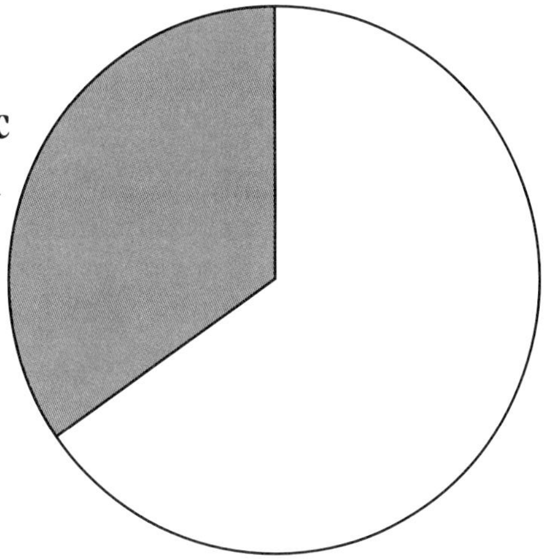

2. List three types of landforms and three water forms on the chart below.

Landforms	Water Forms

3. What is the difference between a globe and a physical map?

____

____

Name ______________________ Date __________

Lesson 2 PAGES 8–13

1. What is a mental map?

___

2. Study the map below of Memorial Park. Answer the following questions.

Memorial Park

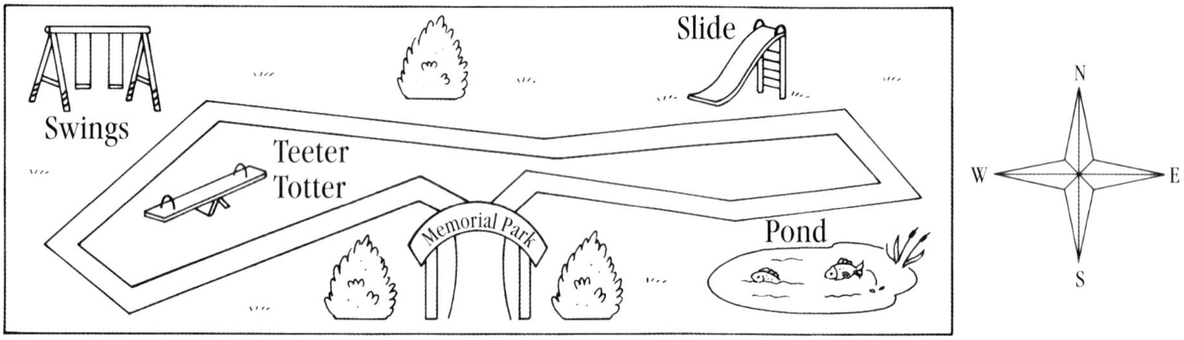

a. Where is the goldfish pond located?

___

b. What kind of things can you do at Memorial Park?

___

___

___

3. Cover up the map of Memorial Park. What do you remember about it? Locate certain things along the walkway. Where is the slide located? Where is the teeter-totter located?

___

___

___

4. Using your mental map, try to draw what you remember about the park on another piece of paper or on the back of this page. Uncover the map when you are finished drawing. Does it look the same? How accurate was your mental map?

Name ____________________ Date __________

Lesson 3 PAGES 14 – 19

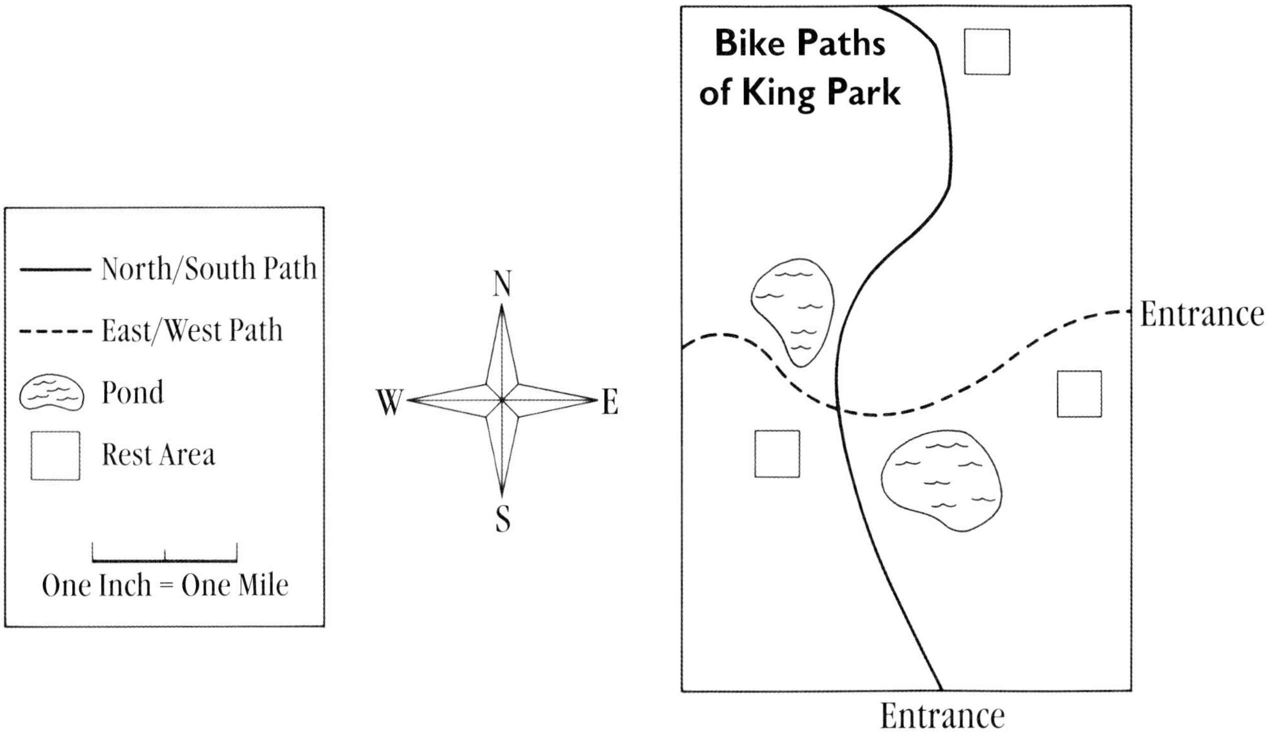

1. How many miles is the North/South Path?

____

2. How many rest areas are there to the east of the North/South entrance?

____

3. If you entered from the East/West entrance, what is the first landmark you would find?

____

4. What is the title of this map?

____

5. How can you tell the difference on the map between the North/South Path and the East/West Path?

____

Name ______________________ Date ____________

Lesson 4 PAGES 20–25

1. What is the name of the map symbol that helps with direction?

____

2. What are the four cardinal directions?

____

3. What are the four intermediate directions?

____

4. Look at the following map of Funland Amusement Park. Answer the questions using intermediate directions.

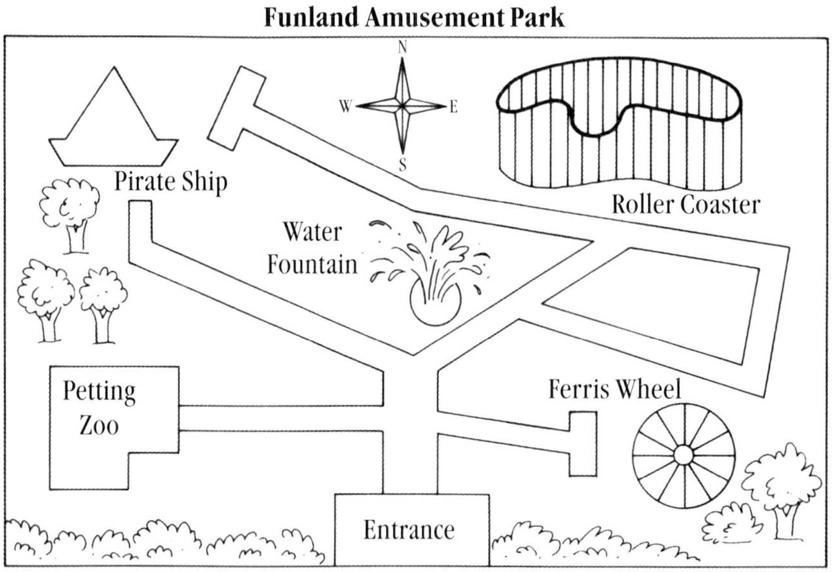

a. If you were standing at the fountain, in what direction would you travel to take a ride on the roller coaster? ______________________

b. After riding on the ferris wheel, in what direction would you travel to ride the pirate ship? ______________________

c. What direction would those people who just arrived have to travel in order to visit the petting zoo? ______________________

Name ______________________ Date __________

Lesson 5 PAGES 26–31

1. A grid map:

a. is a system of lines that form boxes to help people locate places.

b. shows the height of mountains and hills.

c. shows how many people live in an area.

d. does not show where important buildings are in a community.

2. Use the index and the grid map below to answer the following questions.

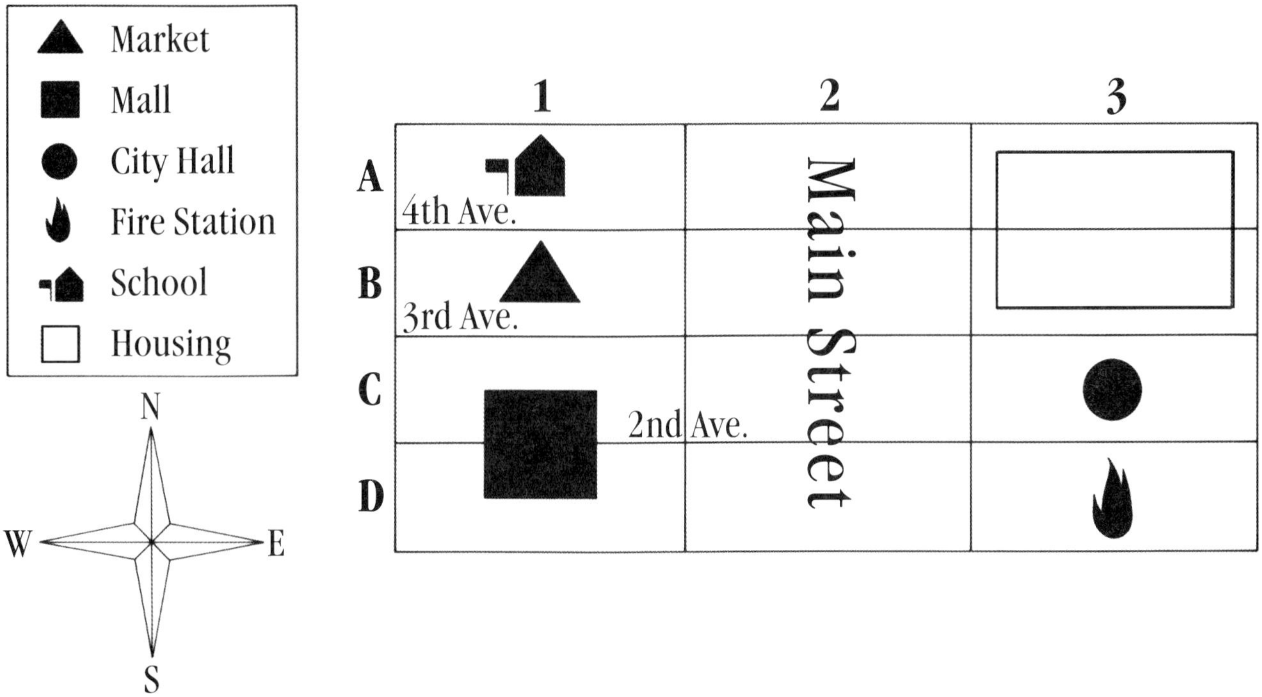

a. What is found at B1? ______________________

b. In what grid boxes is the mall located? ______________________

c. What is on the north side of the market? ______________________

3. In which grid boxes are the following features located?

a. City Hall ______________________

b. Main Street ______________________

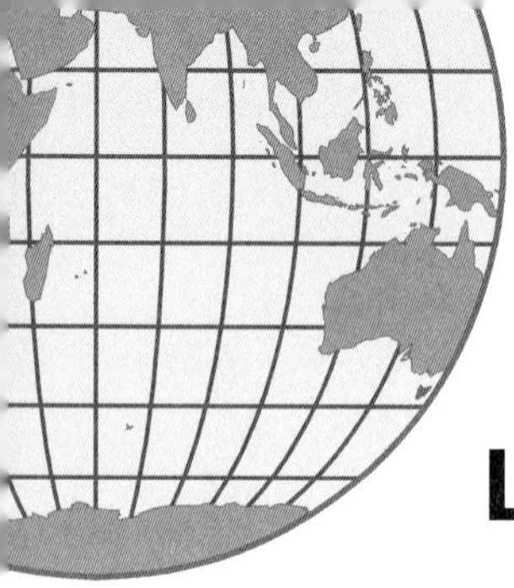

Name ______________________ Date __________

Lesson 6 PAGES 32–37

Pittsburgh, located in western Pennsylvania, and Philadelphia, located in eastern Pennsylvania, are different in many ways. Look at the chart below and answer the following questions about these two cities.

Features	Pittsburgh	Philadelphia
Population	369,879	1,585,577
Area	55.5 square miles	136 square miles
Rivers	Monongahela Allegheny Ohio	Delaware Schuylkill

1. How many people live in

Pittsburgh? ______________________

Philadelphia? ______________________

2. How much land does Pittsburgh cover? ______________________

How much land does Philadelphia cover? ______________________

a. Which has the larger land area, Pittsburgh or Philadelphia? ______________________

b. How much larger is its land area? ______________________

3. What rivers are important to Philadelphia? ______________________

4. What rivers are important to Pittsburgh? ______________________

5. In what ways can a river be important to a city? ______________________

Name ______________________ Date __________

Lesson 7 PAGES 38–43

Answer the following multiple choice questions.

1. A peninsula is:

a. an area of land surrounded by water.

b. an area of land surrounded by water on three sides.

c. a large hill.

2. An island is:

a. an area of land surrounded by water on three sides.

b. an area of land surrounded by water.

c. a large hill.

3. A peninsula was a good location for the new settlement of Jamestown because:

a. many people coming from the Atlantic Ocean could see it and land safely.

b. it could be defended by sea and land.

c. there were not many trees, which allowed for the land to be settled quicker.

4. Jamestown settlers left England because:

a. they were told to leave by King James I because of their religious beliefs.

b. they wanted to sail on newly-designed ships.

c. many hoped to become rich by finding gold and silver.

5. Jamestown was not a good location for a new community because:

a. the land was swampy and the drinking water was full of germs, killing many colonists.

b. the settlers did not know how to get along, and they often fought with each other.

c. it was an island and there was no place for everyone to settle.

Name ______________________ Date ____________

Lesson 8 PAGES 44–49

1. Which items were made by Native American tribes who lived in mountainous areas?

   a. pots, drums, and tepees made from buffaloes

   b. canoes, cornhusk dolls, and wooden homes covered with bark

   c. adobe brick homes and pottery

2. Which Native American tribe used adobe to make their homes?

   a. the Iroquois

   b. the Pueblo

   c. the Sioux

3. What is an artifact?

   ____

   ____

4. What kind of natural resources were available to Native American tribes who lived in the Great Plains?

   ____

   ____

5. What kind of natural resources were available to Native American tribes who lived in the Southwest?

   ____

   ____

Name ______________________ Date ____________

Lesson 9 PAGES 50–55

1. What is a resource?

____

____

2. Describe how the following items can be used as resources for a community.

a. people

b. rivers

c. rich soil

____

____

____

____

____

____

3. Which of the following statements is true about the settling of St. Augustine?

a. St. Augustine was founded by the English so that they could protect their land in the New World.

b. Iron was a valuable resource to the settlers, providing steel for a long-lasting fort.

c. Coquina stone could not be destroyed by fire, allowing a solid fort to be built.

4. St. Augustine is located at a:

a. harbor.

b. mountain side.

c. river.

Name ______________________ Date ____________

Lesson 10 PAGES 56–61

Fill in the blank with the word or phrase below that best completes each sentence.

poultry	map key	soil and climate	fish	wheat and cattle

1. The large ranches in the Plains and the Mountain states often raise

____ .

2. Communities located near lakes, oceans, and rivers often supply

______________________________________ for the country.

3. Small farms in New England raise ____________________________ .

4. Communities decide what products would be best for them to grow or

raise based on ______________________________________ .

5. A ____________________________________ explains the

symbols on a map.

Name ______________________ Date __________

Lesson 11 PAGES 62–67

1. Which of the following statements is true about cities?

a. Many people who live in cities often grow or make items that they need.

b. Major cities that are located on important waterways often become centers where goods are made and can be shipped to other areas.

c. People in rural areas who need jobs do not move to the city.

Look at the following map.

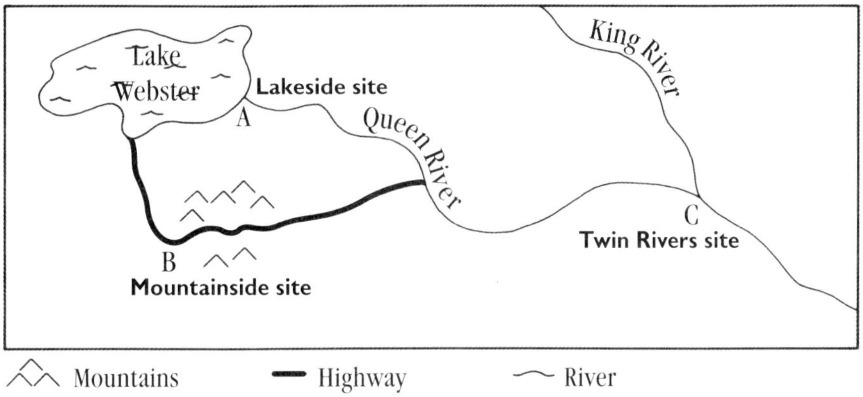

2. Which letter shows the best location for a city? Explain your answer.

a. Lakeside site

b. Mountainside site

c. Twin Rivers site

____

____

3. Which site would have the most trouble developing as a city? Why?

a. Lakeside site

b. Mountainside site

c. Twin Rivers site

____

____

Name ______________________________ Date ______________

Lesson 12 PAGES 68–73

1. A ____________________ is a community of homes located at the edge of a city.

2. What are some of the reasons that suburbs have grown since the 1880s?

3. Which of the following statements is true about suburbs?

a. Suburbs have many industries located in them.

b. More people live in cities than in suburbs.

c. Suburbs have grown because highways and roads have made it easier to travel to and from most cities.

4. How often do people who live in the suburbs go into the city for reasons other than work?

a. often

b. rarely

c. never

Name ____________________ Date __________

Lesson 13 PAGES 74–79

1. Once wheat is planted and harvested, the next step is to transport it to the milling companies. At these milling companies,

a. water, sugar, and yeast are added to make bread dough.

b. the bread is sliced and wrapped.

c. the grain is ground into flour.

2. A machine that helps farmers gather their crops is called a:

a. plow.

b. combine harvester.

c. granary.

3. After wheat is made into flour, it is then transported to:

a. a mill.

b. a grocery store.

c. a bakery.

4. Name two types of wheat.

____________________ ____________________

5. When is spring wheat harvested?

____

Name ______________________ Date ____________

Lesson 14 PAGES 80–85

1. The imaginary line that goes around Earth and divides it into two equal parts is called the:
   - **a.** prime meridian.
   - **b.** equator.
   - **c.** eastern hemisphere.

2. The prime meridian divides Earth into:
   - **a.** eastern and western hemispheres.
   - **b.** northern and southern hemispheres.
   - **c.** the equator.

3. Label the following terms on the diagram below.
   - **a.** prime meridian
   - **b.** northern hemisphere
   - **c.** equator
   - **d.** eastern hemisphere

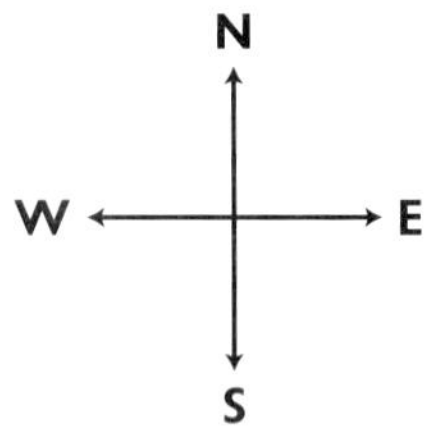

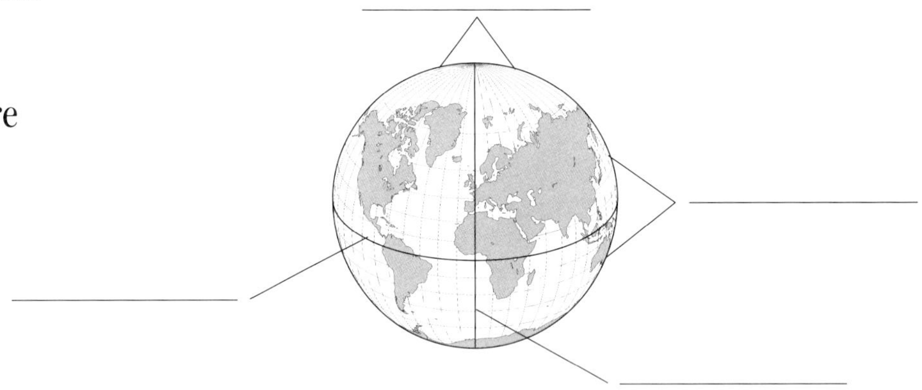

4. The United States is located in what two hemispheres?

____

5. What does it mean when a community is said to be isolated?

____

____

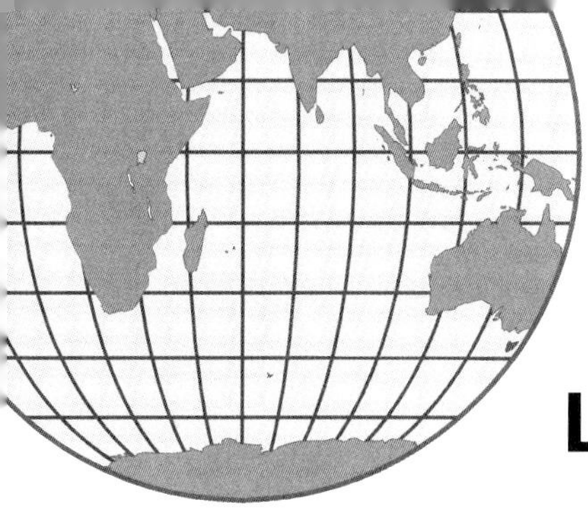

Name ______________________________ Date ______________

Lesson 15 PAGES 86–91

1. Ways of communicating have changed throughout history. Which of the following lists best shows you how communication has changed from the past to the present?

   a. by foot → telegraph → television

   b. television → computer → smoke signals

   c. radio → pony express → movies

2. How did the invention of trains make travel easier?

   ____

   ____

3. Describe how computers have made communication easier.

   ____

   ____

   ____

   ____

4. What kind of physical features were often a problem for early settlers trying to communicate with other settlements?

   ____

   ____

   ____

5. How are physical features overcome today so that people can communicate?

   ____

   ____

   ____

Name ______________________ Date __________

Lesson 16 PAGES 92–97

1. When a new resource is found in an area,

a. more people will be without jobs.

b. population will grow in that area.

c. businesses will close.

d. people will be more likely to move away.

2. How might transportation in a community change when a new resource is found?

____

____

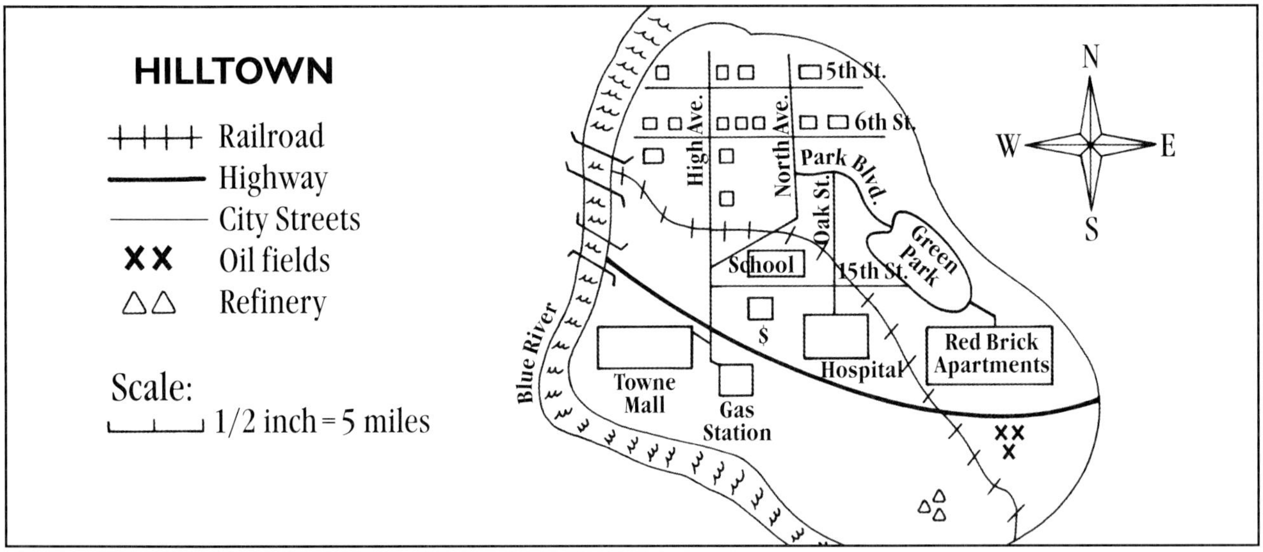

3. Use the map above to answer the following questions about Hilltown.

a. It is ____________ miles from the refinery to the gas station.

b. If a person lives in the Red Brick Apartments in Hilltown, what direction would he travel to get to the mall? ______________

c. Write directions to get to the school from Green Park.

____

____

Name ______________________ Date __________

Lesson 17 PAGES 98–103

1. ______________________ is the process of deepening and widening a waterway.

2. How did dredging the Buffalo Bayou help Houston grow?

____

____

3. When land and water features are made by nature, they are called ______________________ features; when these are built by people, they are called ______________________ features.

4. Describe how the following features could affect a community's growth.

   a. highways

   ____

   ____

   b. mountains

   ____

   ____

   c. rivers

   ____

   ____

   d. airports

   ____

   ____

5. What resource was discovered in 1901 in Texas that helped Houston grow?

____

Name ______________________ Date ____________

Lesson 18 PAGES 104 – 109

1. How did volcanoes form the islands of Hawaii?

____

____

____

____

2. Mauna Loa and Kilauea are:

a. the main islands of Hawaii.

b. two active volcanoes in Hawaii.

c. two kinds of lava.

3. A location near the ______________ and cool ______________ keep Hawaii's temperature pleasant.

4. What physical feature is needed for an area to be in a rain shadow?

____

5. Look at the rain shadow diagram below. Label the following terms.

a. cool winds

b. dry air

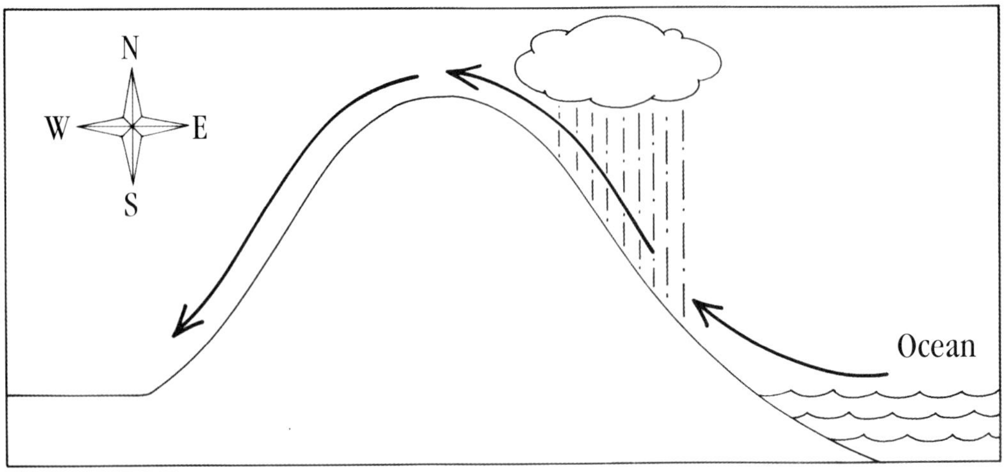